PRAISE FOR GIVING BUSINESS

"A profoundly important book that every business owner must read. It will open your eyes to an exciting and joyful future, and make it remarkably simple to make your business more successful and impactful than you ever dared to imagine."

Steve Pipe, Author of 'The world's most inspiring accountants.'

"As a publisher, writing coach and mentor, I read and work on many excellent books all the time. Giving Business is an outstanding piece of work summarizing and elaborating Masami Sato's change-making vision for the business community. Reading it has inspired me to reframe my own entrepreneurial outlook and relationships with colleagues, clients and partners. I thoroughly recommend any business owner to make use of this gift of a book."

Lucy McCarraher, Author and Publisher. www.rethinkpress.com

"The foundation of a 'Giving Business' is to care more than the competition— to be driven by the difference your business will make in the lives of the people it touches. This is the secret to doing meaningful work. Masami writes from the heart about something she knows and lives every day."

Bernadette Jiwa, International Best-Selling Author

"A real treat to read a business book that is jam-packed full of great and easy to implement ideas, creating remarkable change both within your business and around the world. The unique insights and revolutionary thinking will, help you 'maximize the impact of your life's work while experiencing the maximum sense of enjoyment, gratitude and fulfillment'. A must read if you are looking to make a difference to yourself, team, business and the wider world."

Aynsley Damery, Partner, Tayabali Tomlin

"A compelling book that might just change your meaning of being successful! Giving Business is essential reading for anyone with the purpose of living a truly connected life and business, how to create the most rewarding journey you can ever have, and how to be part of creating a world that you truly want to belong to. Simple, clear and always inspiring, it will change the way you think – at work, at home, every day."

Else Vistisen, Founder of Else Vistisen Therapy

"Masami majestically weaves together the reality of where we are, with our dreams of how the world could be. As a thought leader and action taker in the field of Giving Businesses, she gives practical examples of how to build a business that gives, supports and looks after others without sacrifice or loss. A must read for anyone that cares about the world we leave behind."

Nicholas Haines, Creator of The Vitality Test

Masami provides a powerful, proven roadmap for re-energizing how we do business, make a difference and transform lives. In a world awash with quick fixes, overnight trends and short-term focus, this is hands down the best way I've ever seen to create genuine, sustainable positive impact, woven seamlessly into doing what we already do in our businesses."

Matthew Newnham, Soul Centered Branding Specialist

SEE MORE AT: **WWW.GIVINGBUSINESS.GLOBAL**

GIVING
BUSINESS

MASAMI SATO

Love & Gratitudes

GIVING BUSINESS

BUY1GIVE1 PTE LTD
14 Robinson Road #13-00
Far East Finance Building, Singapore 048545

Ordering Information:
Available at: www.givingbusiness.global
Special discounts are available on quantity purchases by corporations, associations, and others. For details, contact the publisher at the address above.
Please contact: Tel: (+61) 6898-2446; info@b1g1.com;

Printed in Republic of Singapore

First Edition, 2016

ISBN 978-981-09-9245-3

A Buy1GIVE1 Book:
For every five copies of GIVING BUSINESS purchased, one native tree is planted in Borneo to reduce the deforestation effect and help protect Orangutans.

*Find out more **www.b1g1.com***

CONTENTS

FOREWORD

Words matter.

And ever since I've known her, Masami Sato has made words matter more than most.

I frequently tell my friends that she turns my life upside down; she always takes things that I thought were the 'right' way of doing and being, and she replaces them with new, ever-more exciting ways of looking at our world.

And that's precisely what she does for all of us in this great book; she gives us a new way of thinking, being and doing that maximizes the impact each one of us can make in our world. Best of all, perhaps, the words that Masami makes matter are so very simple to act on.

Here, there are no complex business models, no difficult-to-grasp concepts. Instead, you'll find ideas with which we're all totally familiar, but they're expressed in a very unique way; a way that makes them tangible, understandable AND doable.

Masami uses disarming examples like the humble bee (just like the one on the cover of this book) to illustrate profoundly important principles.

Masami operates from a place of humility. Whether she's presenting at a TEDx meeting or in front of any audience, they find her beautifully compelling. And that comes through powerfully in Giving Business.

I believe you'll treasure the time you spend with her in this book. And I believe it triggers something deep inside each one of us so that together, we really can create a happier world.

And that really matters.

Paul Dunn,
Author of the international best-selling book, *The Firm of Future*

CHAPTER 1

INTRODUCTION TO THE JOURNEY

> The real voyage of discovery
> consists not in seeking new landscapes,
> but in having new eyes.
>
> Marcel Proust

A LONG, LONG TIME AGO...

When I was growing up in Japan, I was one of the quietest and shyest children in our neighborhood and at school.

I had trouble expressing my thoughts, ideas and feelings. And whenever I tried to speak in front of others, I somehow couldn't stop my hands from trembling, or hold back my tears. I thought something was wrong with me.

Now, let me go back a little further to explain.

My father lost his father at a young age and grew up in poverty. And he left his home when he was 18 years old, leaving his six siblings and an aging mother behind in pursuit of a better life and more prosperous future. Coming from an underprivileged rural family and having a lower level of education, my father worked very hard to climb the corporate ladder. It was a time when the Japanese economy was starting to boom. Everyone was trying to create a better life.

He was 20 years old when he fell in love with my mother. They married quickly and had my sister and me all within a few years. However, their marriage didn't seem to lead to the happy family life they wanted to create. My mother quit her job to take care of us, and my father's meager income was hardly enough to take care of his growing family's very basic needs.

This financial struggle left my family with little time to spend together.

And much of the conversation that took place around the dinner table was not very positive. Arguments broke out frequently, and I feared that if I didn't behave properly, it would disturb my parents even more, and they would fight again.

Eventually, my family became better off financially (thanks to my dad's hard work), and we were able to afford more things. But the level of happiness and sense of bonding among us didn't seem to improve, no matter how much 'stuff' we possessed. I started to wonder why, and felt that our need to have more was actually compromising our potential for happiness. I thought that many problems in the world, such as poverty and environmental issues, were caused by the businesses that were driving consumerism.

That scared and resentful little child (yes, me) eventually grew up and decided to leave Japan, to try to find the answers to my questions. I wanted to understand the world around me. And despite the fact that I didn't speak English, I started to travel around the world.

Of course, I was scared at first, but through learning to communicate without many words and by connecting with people in simple ways, I started to enjoy expressing myself for the first time in my life.

At that time, I didn't have much to offer. I couldn't speak properly, I didn't have much money and I didn't know anyone in the places I visited. But when I was open and vulnerable, people accepted me for who I was. They generously offered help when I needed it. I didn't feel scared anymore.

That was the first time I started seeing the real beauty of the world and human connection. And it was then that I learned the astonishing power of giving. And one day, I had a life-changing realization.

Actually, we are all the same. We are all trying to create a happier life. We seek to create a better future for our loved ones and ourselves. We all care deeply...

This realization gave me a completely new perspective on what we were all doing. I started to see the problems we had in our world in a very different way. And I realized that businesses were just the vessels powered by these very same people who cared and loved, and had the potential to solve many of the world's problems.

Two decades have passed since then. And I am still committed to my strong beliefs about the powers of giving and connection. These ideas have transformed my life, what I do, and how I perpetuate these values throughout my business.

Today, I'm frequently invited to speak at business events and conferences. I founded and now run a global organization that touches the lives of millions in some of the most meaningful ways.

It's a miracle that this could happen to the little Japanese girl without words.

And today, I'm excited to share with you the simple and powerful insights that will transform your life, your business and the lives of others around you.

Masami

YOUR JOURNEY INSIDE THIS BOOK

As a business person, a leader, an owner, a future CEO—you've probably imagined or believed in making a difference in the world. It's likely that you started doing what you do now so that you could make a significant impact in some way.

Yet, like many others, you've perhaps felt overwhelmed by the scale of the problems and constant challenges we see in the world around us. Many times, what you do at an individual level may not seem to make much of a difference in the grand scheme of things. You also face an increasing number of issues, restrictions and competition in this fast-paced business world we're part of.

It is common knowledge that most businesses fail within their first few years. However, we see many more new ventures beings created year after year. More people than ever before are quitting their secure jobs to start their own businesses. Still others are choosing to work for innovative, smaller businesses with big ideas.

So, if you are one of these daring people, then you must have believed in something very strongly on the day you decided to begin your business venture. It might be that you really wanted to become your own boss. Or you might have felt that you had a special talent and passion for something and wanted to take charge of the expression of your own work. You might have seen a problem that you wanted to solve in a new way. Or you might have discovered an excellent opportunity that you thought no one else had ever spotted…

This book is written for you and for people who are business owners, entrepreneurs, directors and managers, or those who want to lead their own lives, their teams and their business directions powerfully.

There is a difference, however. This book is not just about how to become *successful* in the traditional sense. It's about broadening that success to include leading a truly *connected* life and business, creating the most rewarding journey you could ever have, and becoming part of creating a world in which you actually want to belong.

This book also gives you insights from the journey I've been on to find the real key to creating Giving Businesses with maximum impact and meaning.

Nearly two decades ago, I ventured into the world of small businesses. And at one point, I was a business owner and mother of two young children, running around to grow my own business (you'll find out more about this later). We started that business so that we could be doing something great, and at the end of the day, give back to help people who had little. I wanted to be a small help to those who had fewer opportunities while finding my own life purpose and enjoying everything along the way.

That eventually led to the formation of the global giving initiative, Buy1GIVE1 (B1G1) in 2007. At that time, I realized that there were many business owners like me who also wanted to make meaningful contributions, but found it hard to do anything about it because they were stretched too thin.

I wanted to create a mechanism to make it easy and impactful for businesses to give back so that they could all make a difference each and every day, no matter what stage of business development they were in.

Today, B1G1 helps companies around the world give back and make a difference through their own unique *Giving Stories*.

Imagine a cafe providing access to life-saving water for every coffee they sell, or an accounting firm helping educate a child in need for every client they serve, or an author planting a tree for every book sold...

We make these things (and so much more) happen every day; thanks to all the business people who jumped on board to do something very different—to create a world that's full of giving.

During the developmental years of this initiative, we've worked with countless businesses, non-profit organizations and people in a variety of professions. We've learned priceless lessons, and gradually developed processes and systems that pushed us forward. To date, more than 1,500 small-to-medium sized businesses from all industries globally have joined us and have collectively created more than 78 million giving impacts (as of May 2016). While there is much more to be done, we can say that we have achieved something special together.

And ultimately, that's what this book is about; helping you achieve something special too.

I want you to live the most meaningful life you can possibly live. And I believe that the ideas and insights shared in this book will help you maximize your impact in this new meaning-driven world around us. It will remind you of the real power of giving and of how embedding a strong focus on giving in your business can transform you and your business.

As you start to put the ideas here into action, you will certainly experience the feeling of making a difference. Then you will start seeing people around you being more positively impacted by your actions, your words and your attitude.

You will experience more clarity and ease in making decisions, and you will feel even more connected to the things you do and to the people with whom you interact. You will produce results in new ways, and you will experience an increased sense of satisfaction throughout your business endeavors. And most importantly, you will experience the real power within you.

I hope you will choose to spread these positive impacts to many others in business around you too.

Because businesses with a real sense of purpose really can change our world.

YOUR REAL WIN: IT'S JUST A GAME

Before we move into the main contents of this book, we have one important question to clarify together; *what defines your success; your real win?*

What's Your Real Win?

So… what are you really looking for in your life? What is your ultimate goal in business? What is your life all about? These are the big questions.

You probably have special aims and goals that are different from what other people are trying to achieve. And these specific goals might change over time too. So, what is your **ultimate** goal?

I tend to think that the easiest way to form a clearer perspective of what life really is about and why we do what we do is to use a simple metaphor like this:

Living life and running a business is like a game.

Yes, one of the key objectives of your life, your business and a game you play can be to win; to experience great outcome. We all enjoy accomplishing great things and achieving our goals.

However, there is much more to this. I see that there are three key points that our lives, our businesses and any game we play have in common. And they are often overlooked.

1. There is a Beginning and an End

Very simply, any game has a beginning and an end. At some point in time, we chose to begin playing a game. And no matter how much fun we have, we eventually need to finish playing the game.

Similarly, our lives have a beginning and an end.

No matter how different we are, we all came from our parents. Our lives had different, yet very similar beginnings. We were just infants with no knowledge about the world around us when we were born.

And no matter how hard we try, we cannot escape death. We cannot buy immortality.

Businesses are the same. Every business starts with a thought. It's the moment a business is born. Then there comes a time when the business transforms into something else, or it's no longer needed because the times have changed.

Some of the oldest recorded businesses that we have in our world today are several hundred years old (more on this later). These businesses outlive any one of us because businesses can be handed down generation to generation, from person to person. But even businesses cannot escape from their endings. Put another way; they are not meant to stay in a particular state forever.

Businesses exist to solve problems, serve people and create value. So, when people's needs change, businesses (or their products and services) have to adjust accordingly.

2. There are Rules You Follow

Whether we like it or not, there are rules to follow in life, in business and in games. We learn to follow certain rules, try to set up new ones and try breaking some of them to see what happens...

The rules we have can change as we progress. Some rules are written or regulated; others are more like moral values or superstitions. The fact is that there are rules everywhere whether you like them or not, and knowing the destinations, objectives and important rules to follow makes the journey much easier and more meaningful.

In the game of life and business, we are continuously on the lookout for new tips, new rules and new insights so that we can become better players. The more aware we are of the game we are playing and the rules we need to follow, the clearer we feel about the game as a whole. After all, the rules only exist to make the experience of playing a game better for everyone.

But the third and final point that is common in our lives, businesses and games is the most critical one. Because understanding this point makes all the difference...

3. The Real Objective: To Enjoy

When we play a game, we can be so consumed in the experience that we may forget the fact that the real aim of the game is to simply enjoy. It is easy to become too focused on outcomes.

Picture a group of children playing a game and imagine a child throwing a tantrum because he/she is losing. Alternatively, picture a child cheating and annoying everyone else in the group.

We might see these as just innocent and common child behaviors. However, the reality is that many adults also play the game of life/ business in the same manner. Some go into emotional turmoil with every little incident and negatively affect the people around them. Some try to cut corners in their business practices at other people's expenses. Some ignore the agreed rules secretly or deceive others so that they can have better outcomes for themselves. Many believe that the **ultimate** aim of life/business is to…win.

Beyond Winning

What matters more is what happens **after** winning or losing. Would others celebrate and rejoice in your win with you? Would they come to support you in times of difficulty? Do you feel as motivated to get back on track after a big failure? Do you feel grateful and satisfied when you experience a win? And how long does that sense of satisfaction last?

The game of life and business has many ups and downs just like all other games. Both winning and losing are just a part of the game. Because we don't always win (there are often more losses than wins), we enjoy the experience of winning even more. Because of our own losses, we understand the feelings of others who have difficulties.

One day, there will be an end to the game you are currently playing. On the day you finish your game, would you like to feel satisfied and grateful? Or regretful, sad and angry? If you agree that the former is the way you want to feel every day until the day you finish your game, please read on and put the ideas in this book into practice.

Please remember that your definition of success (the aim of your game) now involves two elements; to accomplish the great things you actually desire AND to feel fulfilled throughout the entire process. Once you are clear about your true win, this book will help you find the path to your real success: both in business and in life. I guarantee that you will see, feel and experience the positive impact.

After all, you are the one to experience your real win in your game: the true success of your life and business. And most importantly, you'll enjoy the journey itself, much more than ever.

THRIVING IN A MEANING-DRIVEN WORLD

The Invention of Businesses

When the oldest forms of businesses (trades) were created more than 10,000 years ago, our aim was to exchange what we had with what we didn't have to fulfill our basic needs.

Through these trades, what you could not collect or produce could be obtained from others in exchange for what you had. Some people wanted to have what you had, and they had something you wanted. The value exchange of trading/bartering made perfect sense. It was a win-win model.

When standardized currencies emerged, they made these exchanges easier and more efficient because money didn't perish the way food did and it was easy to carry and count. And with this newly found convenience, we also started to accumulate the surplus to build greater wealth for ourselves and our offspring.

Money became something much more than what we used for the convenience of simple exchanges. It became a token for our future security.

Eventually, our aspiration for creating ever greater wealth and abundance has lead to our modern day business model that focuses on the maximization of profits as the most important Key Performance Indicator (KPI) of today's business development. We have lived in a profit-driven world. Many thought that the more profit we made each year, the happier and prouder we would become.

The Widening Gap

The reality is that there is actually no end to our desire to have more. When we have enough for our own survival and comfort, we naturally start wanting other things. This can be a great thing as it creates opportunities for more businesses, more jobs, and more economic prosperity. But some businesses in our world eventually became very powerful, arguably too powerful, even more powerful than some countries. Therefore, the way these huge companies operate their businesses has enormous impact, for better or for worse.

Today the gap between the 'rich' and 'poor' is widening. In 2015, the Organization for Economic Cooperation and Development (OECD) announced that (in its 34 member states) the richest 10 percent of the population earned 9.6 times the income of the poorest 10 percent.[1] According to a report published by Oxfam in the same year, the world's wealthiest 62 people are claimed to possess as much wealth as the poorest 3.6 billion people around the planet.[2]

That's astonishing.

A large percentage of the world's population is struggling to survive and sustain itself because available resources are not circulated to benefit everyone. Yet more and more natural resources are extracted from our planet every day—far more than what's actually needed. And much of the excess is discarded as waste or stored away for the perceived future security of the few.

Ironically, many of those who have access to this 'overabundance' are negatively impacted by it because excessive consumption can harm us.

For example, one billion people today are overweight and at risk of developing serious diseases while another one billion (or more) struggle to have even basic nutrition to survive.

This is far from an efficient use of the resources of our world. It seems quite clear that improving the way our economic power is distributed and utilized would benefit everyone more. One factor holding us back could be our singular focus on financial gain.

The Profit-Driven Economy

When we are solely focused on the maximization of profits in our economy, there are two things for us to do; to increase revenue (the incoming flow of funds) or to reduce expenses (the outgoing flow of funds).

To increase and maximize revenue, businesses became smarter and more effective in their communication approach. In the world of marketing, clever advertising could be used to induce people's desire to have things even when they don't really need them. And with the strong focus to simply sell more, some businesses have even made bigger promises than what they could deliver. Making more sales quickly meant more profit, and more profit meant success.

To minimize expenses, businesses started seeking more ways to further reduce their costs. From time to time, we've seen the downsides of these cost reduction practices. These approaches included 'paying less to the people who were desperate to get jobs even in inhumane working conditions' or 'dumping toxic waste into the ground or the waterways because it was cheaper to do so than to treat it properly'. The decisions leading to these challenges were often made without the knowledge of potential consequences. But sometimes they were made knowingly too because reducing cost today meant more profit tomorrow. And more profit, again, meant success.

In many of the largest corporations, managers and CEO's who were able to maximize short-term profits were highly sought after and rewarded. In contrast, the leaders who tried to create longer-term results risked their positions by trying to prioritize the well-being of workers or environmental sustainability if they were unable to produce the massive short-term profits the investors wanted to see.

While making profits is undeniably integral for businesses so that they can grow and scale, prioritizing profits alone has created many unintended consequences.

The Inevitable Change

The singular focus on the profit-driven business model started to show flaws in the latter part of the 20ᵗʰ century. We discovered that there was a limited amount of natural resources we could extract from this planet. We saw that there was only so much toxic waste we could bury on our land and in our water sources before many of us started to get sick. And the question was: *"Who should be responsible for dealing with it?"*

We thought that our governments should do something about it. We've blamed corporations for making all the evil decisions and hoarding the wealth. And we've expected advancing technologies to take care of it.

But today, more and more people acknowledge that it is, in fact, all of us who can and must do something about this to protect the desired future for our children.

It's still easy to close our eyes to the problems and say, *"There is no point in making the effort to change because everyone else is doing it. I can't change the world alone."*

However, that's not an option anymore. We **know** that we have the power to create change. And today, it is possible for individuals, especially business owners, to influence our world immensely because of the power of the connectedness we now have through advanced technology.

There has never been a time like this.

The Meaning-Driven World

Today, nearly half the world uses the internet, and Facebook alone has 1.5 billion active monthly users (that's about 20% of the world population).[3] And remarkably, the number of people who use a mobile phone is greater than the number of people who use a toilet...[4] It's undeniable that we are becoming highly connected across the globe and are continuously seeking ways to connect even more.

In this connected world, the way businesses succeed is changing rapidly too. Businesses can hide fewer things today. When they mistreat their workers, the stories can go viral much quicker. When they breach ethical codes, they can easily be exposed online. Today's customers and employees have greater choices and access to real and fair information. Many people no longer buy things just because they need them and they don't work for companies just because they need the income. Now, more and more people are consciously starting to buy things from companies whose values and missions resonate directly and personally with them.

The *2015 Cone Communication/Ubiquity Global CSR Study* reflects the sentiments of nearly 10,000 citizens in nine of the largest countries in the world by GDP: the United States, Canada, Brazil, the United Kingdom, Germany, France, China, India and Japan. Researchers found that nine out of 10 consumers expected companies to do more than make a profit, and also operate responsibly to address social and environmental issues. And 84 percent of consumers globally said that they sought out responsible products whenever possible, though 81 percent cited availability of these products as the largest barrier to not purchasing more.[5]

Consumers aren't just saying that they care about company values—their actions and buying history is reflecting this shift.

Recent studies also confirm that people are also starting to look for more meaning in their jobs. According to a study done by Clark University, 78 percent of established adults (25-39 years olds) say it is more important to enjoy work than to make a lot of money and 82 percent of them say it is important to have a career that does some good in the world.[6]

The new world we are starting to create is a meaning-driven world. We seek reasons for our actions, our relationships and our existence. People are starting to be more willing to pay more for the things they believe in, or even take a smaller paycheck for doing the work they are passionate about.

So, for businesses to survive and thrive in this new world, we need to play the game with a new set of rules.

What you learn in the following chapters will enhance your ability to thrive in this new *meaning-driven* world. That is, as you'll discover, a happier world.

CHAPTER 2

CREATING A GIVING BUSINESS

Every person has a longing to be significant;
to make a contribution; to be a part of
something noble and purposeful.

John C. Maxwell

WHAT WE LEARN FROM THE BEES

In this chapter, we explore how to design and create a Giving Business.

On a fundamental level, a Giving Business is a business that offers three key things: great value and meaning for you (owner); great value and meaning for your stakeholders (team, investors, customers); great value and meaning for the society and the world.

And as we begin the journey into the concept of Giving Business, let me introduce you to something smaller and simpler. A bee. Actually, a colony of bees.

The reason we start this important chapter with these tiny insects is that they are actually nature's expert in creating great Giving Enterprises.

Now, let me take you into the world of bees.

The Successful Colony Decoded

In his book '*THE WISDOM OF BEES*', Michael O'Malley Ph.D., a social psychologist and executive editor at Yale University Press, points out the similarities between prosperous bee colonies and successful human enterprises.[7] His work provides some fascinating insights for us to look at.

Dr. O'Malley's journey into the world of bees started when he took up a "*nice little hobby*" to share with his son; bee-keeping. And to his surprise, he started to see very specific and consistent behaviors in the bee colony. He observed behaviors that made the groups work together in a remarkably coordinated effort to achieve a common goal: a goal that was more than just to make honey.

Those behaviors are, as Dr. O'Malley points out, the secret to the bee's success.

Now, you probably know quite a lot about the structural similarities between bee colonies and human societies already. In bee colonies (similar to other ant and insect colonies), individuals work together in their distinct roles to support the growth of their kind. And these insects that form large colonies dominate the insect world against all other insects that act alone.

According to Dr. O'Malley, one of the qualities bees demonstrate that might not exist in many human organizations is the consistent and collective long-term focus on true sustainability.

> "Bees don't focus exclusively on the most productive flower patches at any given time, and for good reason. Conditions change rapidly for bees and they can ill afford wide swings in pollen and nectar intake. What is best now probably won't be tomorrow. In the animal kingdom, the famine in 'feast or famine' is a death sentence. Thus, when a lucrative vein of nectar is discovered, the entire colony doesn't rush to mine it no matter how enriching the short-term benefits.... Said succinctly, bees avoid all-or-nothing scenarios at all cost."

Listening to these insights from the bee 'kingdom' makes you wonder why human organizations and businesses have failed to see such simple fundamentals.

When companies have a long-term focus, their perspectives widen beyond trying to maximize quarterly profit figures.

A long-term focus means caring for the harmonious co-existence of our race. And understanding the delicate balance between short-term wins and the long-term implications allows us to design strategies and actions that make a real difference.

Giving Back by Design

Bees naturally give back too. They don't need to have a CSR department or external expectations and pressure to do the right things.

Researchers who study bees tell us that a single bee colony can pollinate as many as 300 million flowers every day (yes, every day). Bees naturally create their own abundance automatically through what they do every day. Their giving happens by design, and it is an integral part of their existence.

Bees are so small. We might not think that they impact our world so much. Yet, if we look more closely into what's happening, we will discover that 30 percent of the fruits and vegetables we eat require honeybees to pollinate them. A staggering 90 percent of our nutritional intake comes from foods that require pollination.[8] It means that the 'giving back' conducted by bees has a far greater impact on our world than we imagine.

This also means that when bees and other insects stop pollinating, scarcity becomes inevitable. And sadly, it is already starting to happen in many parts of our world. In the U.S. alone, the number of bee colonies per 10,000 square meters has declined by a staggering 90 percent since 1962. Overuse of insecticide in large-scale agriculture and other industrial developments are often blamed for the massive decline in bee populations.

The methods we use today to extract more resources with less time and costs for our own short-term gain (maximization of short-term profit) are playing a part in causing these special insects to disappear. It almost looks like we are driving ourselves towards famine.

So, what can we be doing now?

The Natural Cycles

In our world, there are cycles we live with. All natural things follow these cycles to create greater flow and abundance. These include the cycle of seasons, planetary cycles, movement of time and our life cycles. If you try to change these cycles or do things to counteract them, you require much more energy to thrive, or you may even end up developing more problems.

If you are a farmer, you plan your work around the seasons. You're well aware that you can only successfully grow plants that are suited to those seasons (unless you use greenhouses and various chemicals). You know that certain plants are suited to the weather, climate and soil of your region while others are not. You also know that you cannot simply grow the same kind of plants on the same land year after year without putting anything back into the soil.

Just like the bees, traditional farmers know how to live with these cycles and how to give back. They think about the long-term. And they can be largely in control of producing a great harvest.

So, by stepping back and learning to understand the cycles we live and work with, business owners like you can start designing businesses that embrace the power of those cycles and mechanisms of abundance.

One of the barriers preventing us from achieving this is the decline of real wisdom in our world.

Declining Wisdom

Before we had technology to alter the natural cycles and other conditions, we simply found ways to improve our methods so that we could live more seamlessly with the cycles that existed. We started handing down the knowledge and wisdom we gained to the next generation through our own stories of successes and painful failures. Wise elders in communities were highly respected and consulted when important decisions were to be made.

At some point, as the development of technology changed at an astonishing speed such as we had never seen before, we started to lose our respect for the wisdom of our elders.

Our decisions can be made through a quick online search based on how others rate things. We don't really need to remember people's names, faces and contact details because we have them stored on our phones.

And we don't need to take much time (and care) to develop relationships because we have so many online 'friends' and we can keep creating more. Consequently, connections have become disposable.

We also don't need to spend time learning about specific topics because we can find the best expert knowledge and insights online. So, the need to acquire and retain knowledge has become disposable too.

Our blind spot though is ignoring our heavy dependence on technology. We can easily assume that future technologies can solve all our current and upcoming problems. But if we suddenly lose access to the tools and resources; the infrastructure and the knowledge base we are so used to tapping into, what can we actually do to sustain our lives? When our external situations change dramatically, some of our most useful tools could become outdated and even useless.

Wisdom, on the other hand, doesn't get affected by external conditions as much. It can be applied in many different situations at any point in time. Dictionaries define *wisdom* as '*the ability to think and act using knowledge, experience, understanding, common sense, and insight.*'

Wisdom + Technology = Accelerated Positive Impact

Having great wisdom combined with the access to great technologies can be very powerful. And businesses can also benefit from building a great 'wisdom base' in their enterprises. When times change, businesses with wisdom can find new ways to thrive while businesses without wisdom that were previously doing well because of a specific trend can easily become outdated in the process of a major external change.

The bee colony observed by Dr. O'Malley didn't focus on harvesting the most amount of nectar by going for the most prosperous flower patch altogether, no matter how great the short-term gain was. They knew the consequences of a short-term focus. The wisdom of the bees is naturally handed down through the generations. Left to their own devices without human influence, bees will continue to thrive as they continue to pollinate the flowers and maintain their own sustainable habits. They show us that we can also live in harmony with the great wisdom our ancestors and predecessors have left for us.

Wisdom in business is a power that does not get outdated no matter what happens externally. It gives us the ability to thrive long-term by staying in touch with the natural cycles.

Now, let's see some examples of businesses with great wisdom; businesses that last.

THE SECRET OF FAMILY BUSINESS

Challenges of Being a 'Boss'

In the profit-driven business world, it's easy to perceive your team, your suppliers and your marketplace as tools for your business to make more money. However, this perception leads you to a very lonely playing field.

In fact, many business owners have mentioned to me that they find it hard now to get a great level of commitment and dedication from their teams.

People in business are more likely to feel isolated in the competitive business environment when they see 'winning' as the ultimate goal. Some feel disillusioned by their partners and suppliers because (from their own perspectives) their partners and suppliers didn't deliver on the promises they made.

When we focus on making money as the highest priority, it's easy to perceive that everyone else is 'only looking out for themselves,' trying to take advantage of each other.

When the current bosses were employees themselves, they had other colleagues to associate with at an equal level. But once they became the employers, the journey became harder and lonelier for many of them. On top of that, they now have so many competitors, heavy responsibilities and distractions. No wonder the journey of a business owner can be very overwhelming.

Lack of Trust—the Biggest Threat to Business

Some of these business owners are also afraid that if they increase their prices, their customers and clients will leave them and do business elsewhere. But by keeping prices low to retain business, they have to compromise on some aspects of their offerings. And many of them even end up becoming the least paid-per-hour team members in their companies (if they ever divided their salaries by the hours they work).

No matter how tough it sounds, the struggles of these business owners actually start with their own perceptions and beliefs.

On the other side of the spectrum, employees of these companies could be feeling that their companies are merely using them to make more money; they do not think that their companies care enough about them. If you look at the Gallup 2015 survey, it indicates that a staggering 87 percent of employees worldwide are not engaged at work. And their research shows that managers account for at least 70 percent of variance in employee engagement scores in the companies.[9]

The customers of these businesses tend to focus on the price, speed and quality of their products and services because that's the only way for them to make sense of buying from them.

It's easy to get trapped in this dilemma as a business owner because, in reality, everyone is selfish. People usually do what they do to benefit themselves and their loved ones. Yet, we also need to be reminded that these same individuals can be moved to do things voluntarily and selflessly too—things that go far beyond their own personal gains. When trusted, inspired and appreciated, people do amazing things.

Businesses that create a greater sense of trust and a stronger sense of connection with their employees and customers can commit to their values with confidence, genuine caring and clarity. And they provide more than tangible benefits. They provide **meaning**.

And these businesses tend to outlive the ones that fail to form real trusting relationships with their stakeholders.

The Longevity of Businesses

The lifespan of businesses today is shrinking. In the 1970s, the average lifespan of large corporations in US (businesses in the S&P 500 list) was 27 years. This is steeply down from 75 years in the 1920s. And in the last decade, it further declined to a mere 15 years.

In parallel, the average tenure of a CEO has fallen sharply as well. In the 1970s, the average CEO held his position for almost 12 years. But this has almost halved to an average tenure of just six years.

Here, we can see that the shortened tenure of leadership may have some kind of impact on the shortened lifespan of businesses.

Average Tenure of CEO and Lifespan of Companies [10]

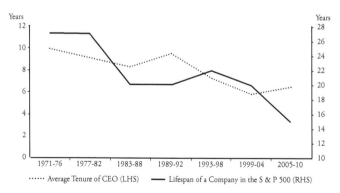

As of September 2014
Source: Conference Board, Foster
Universe based upon companies within the S&P 500 index

Longevity of business is an important subject to anyone who is starting and driving a business aiming to create any lasting impact; *how can my business thrive long-term?*

Let's find an answer to that.

It is little-known that more than 50 percent of the world's oldest and still operational businesses are Japanese businesses. There are more than 20,000 companies that are more than 100 years old in Japan. According to the Guinness Book of Records, some of these businesses are more than several hundred years old.[11] Considering that the population of Japan is only less than two percent of the world's population, this is a remarkable finding.

When you delve deeper into this, you will discover something interesting and significant: in Japan, many businesses tend to continue generation after generation because they are owned and operated by families. And this happens because of the strong sense of commitment the members of the family have to each other and to the *legacy* of family they all share.

So, at first glance, it looks like forming a family business is the key to ensuring the longevity of the business.

But this is not the full picture; even family ties come to a halt when the descendants do not reproduce or when they decide not to inherit the family business. And even if there are people who can inherit the business, they might not be capable of running it. This is how most family businesses eventually cease to exist.

The reason why Japanese family businesses tend to last longer than those in other countries is because it's quite common for these Japanese families to even 'adopt' talented and dedicated adult outsiders so that the business can still continue as a family business even when there is no one in the direct family to inherit it. They maintain the *structure* of a family business even when there is no family member to carry it on.

Think about it this way: the insights we gain from Japan's family businesses suggest that we have a better chance to create a business that lasts by establishing a business environment/structure that *resembles* a family model.

In this way, we harness the benefits of both models; the longevity of the family business model and the freedom of the non-family business model that elects its own leaders based on the required qualities beyond a family tie.

Let's look at how we can actually create family-like businesses to take advantage of these insights.

The Secret of Family-Run Businesses

Here are some secrets of thriving family businesses:

Secret 1: Trust is everything.
People trust each other more naturally in family businesses. This helps them achieve great feats even in difficult times.

They also care as much about the relationships with their suppliers and customers as their own business. Taking care of their social ties is more than just important to them because the aim of the business is to last for a long time for their descendants.

Everyone in the business understands that trust is the most valuable asset that an enterprise can and must have. And creating trust becomes ingrained in the shared mission amongst all family members.

Secret 2: Everyone feels rewarded by working towards a collective goal.

In great family businesses, all members care about how to contribute more; to serve the business in the best way by growing the reputation together. They are not thinking about exchanging their time for money.

When anyone in the family is sick or disabled, taking care of that person becomes the shared responsibility of the family and the business too. It means that there is an inherent sense of security and belonging in the business environment.

And they celebrate their wins together without trying to take credit for their own individual efforts and achievements.

Secret 3: The power of giving back is never neglected.

In family businesses, people understand and share the same moral values. Therefore, contributing to the community they belong to is a critical responsibility for them.

They realize that all their successes are made possible by the social ties and natural environment to which they belong, and that giving back is more than their responsibility.

Just like traditional farmers, they know the importance of taking care of the soil of their land to receive abundant harvest.

These secrets reveal that family businesses are fundamentally driven by the wisdom they have cultivated. They think of the long-term consequences of their actions today regarding the gifts they leave for their descendants for many generations.

As special as they may seem, the characteristics that make great family businesses are simply practical ways of thinking that create greater, lasting success.

Any business can adopt this way of thinking even if they are not family-run businesses. The question you might have is, *"How do we do that in our business while still making money?"*

Here's the answer: we just need to *think* like a family.

Thinking Like a Family

Mother Teresa once said, **"The problem with the world is that we draw our family circle too small."**

To many, 'family' means those people with whom we have blood ties.

But it also includes the people our direct relatives are married to. Sometimes people adopt children, or choose to have *family* pets. And family ties can be formed through agreements and choices too.

Also, consider this: these days, most people spend more time with their colleagues than with their families. Therefore, how people feel while surrounded by the people they work with has a significant influence on the happiness level of these individuals.

It's common sense that having happy employees has a significant impact on the bottom-line of the company, so it's astonishing that many businesses today still make hiring choices without considering whether the new hire really fits in with the culture of the company. Productivity is often valued more than the emotional and energetic contribution of employees, and far less attention is given to making the team feel connected.

Now, of course, non-family businesses have a significant advantage over family businesses in one aspect. They don't need to worry about the challenges that many family businesses have: the lack of real talent within the available candidates. If only family members are permitted to fulfill the management (or other skilled) roles and assume the ownership, what happens when no one in the family is suited for these positions? A family business, no matter how great it has been, can clearly fail when they do not find the right successors.

Commercial enterprises have a great advantage in this area because they can recruit more people with real talent and promote the right people to critical leadership positions.

There is no shortage of talent in the talent pool beyond the family. And you can even headhunt talented people from other high-performing companies.

But the most challenging part of all is to find the *right* people and to establish trusting, growth-focused long-term relationships with them.

Consider, for example, what happened when Forbes Magazine interviewed the CEOs of top performing companies about the major challenges their companies faced. They found that most common challenge cited was *"attracting the right talents"* and *"building the highest-performing teams"*.[12]

Now let's see how we can tackle this challenge by combining the strength of both family business and non-family business.

Making Hiring Choices as a Family Business

When we attract people who have great capabilities and great attitudes, they produce far greater results than when we have twice as many people who are talented yet not engaged or who are passionate yet don't have the right capabilities and qualities.

Of course, the worst case is when you hire people who do not have a good attitude and are not even capable in the appointed role. As you'll see in the chart below, it's simple to identify what kinds of people you should avoid hiring, but most of us in business have made this very simple mistake in the past.

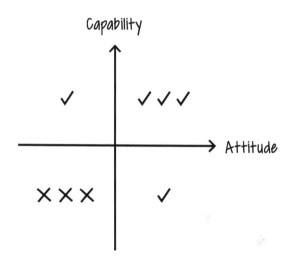

This diagram shows that the aim is to find those who have three or more ticks.

But many businesses end up hiring more people with one tick than people with three ticks. And that's because individuals with three or more ticks are likely to be doing well already and enjoying their current work.

At any one time, the majority of those who are looking for jobs are either the ones who are dissatisfied with the previous/current work or who are not valued and appreciated by their previous/current employers.

The chances of finding 'three-tick people' by placing an advertisement is quite slim. Finding the right match is tough unless you are lucky, offer a lot of flexibility (but not necessarily financial benefits), or alternatively, have a very special message to share; a message or purpose that becomes a magnet for precisely the right people.

No matter how you're trying to find the right people, the most important thing is that you run the selection process as if you're setting out to find new *family members.*

If you were considering these candidates to be part of your family, would you hire them? This decision is as important as finding the right marriage partner because once you've made the choice, your company is going to spend lots of time with the new hire. And more than just the time itself, the energy of these new team members will influence the entire team's dynamics and represent your company's identity.

Most important of all, the reason for you to find the right new family members is not because you make more money as a result, but because you want to ensure that these new and talented individuals will thrive and positively influence your business...your family.

Having people who are motivated, inspired and appreciated transforms the culture of your business and uplifts others to be the best they can be. On the other hand, having a person who has lower standards can bring down the overall standard of the entire team too.

Great hiring decisions cannot be made when you merely see the new employee as another cog in the wheel.

That's because what you don't appreciate does not appreciate.

Growing a Team as a Family Business.

As a business leader, your job is not to just get a job done. It is to drive the uplifting, engaging, harmonious and trusting environment in *the family*. You are the one to take care of everyone in your family as a guardian and create more leaders who can do that too.

To become a good guardian, you have to be great at setting clear boundaries, standing with distinct values, encouraging others to make significant efforts while trusting, caring and loving the members just like great parents do. And you'd also be interested in finding ways to help members of your family grow and live fulfilling lives because it's ultimately necessary for the business to have happy and thriving employees.

Caring about the personal growth and work satisfaction of each team member is far more important than just focusing on how many financial and other job benefits you offer to attract and retain talent. If the reason people stay in your company is for those benefits alone, you will still struggle to keep them. Not only that, you'll find it challenging to encourage them to give more than expected. And the moment you are no longer able to offer greater incentives, you will lose the people you've invested so much in.

Surprisingly perhaps, when you dig deeper in this, you discover that many of the Fortune 500 companies have very high employee turnover rates. In addition to this, a survey by *Payscale* revealed that employee tenure does not increase according to increased salaries.

Take a look at the '*Companies with the Most & Least Loyal Employees (2013)*'. When you do, you'll discover that Google and Amazon appear on the top 5 of the 'least loyal' side of that list.[13] And in the same report, you'll also find that they were offering salaries that were much higher than the industry standards. So, the reason people were leaving would not be because of a lack of financial incentives.

You'd think that being hired by companies like Google would be like landing a dream job (Google has been rated highly on the '*FORTUNE's 100 BEST COMPANIES TO WORK FOR*' list for the past 10 years). But if many of their employees are leaving so fast, the reality of working for Google or Amazon probably did not exceed the high expectations these people had when they decided to join these companies.

Offering more *meaning*, even with fewer benefits, might help you attract the right people and retain them. It's amazing how you can attract high quality people as volunteers or interns when you are not even offering any financial incentives. This is because the reason they come to work for you and with you is for something more: meaning.

And if you cared about your employees as much as you cared about your family, you'd be having different conversations, placing different expectations and holding different thoughts about them.

The tangible rewards you offer are not the catch to hold on to the talent. They are for appreciating the contributions your team members are making. If you really see them as part of your family, you'd definitely want to see them succeed and prosper. And you'd be sharing your hopes and aspirations with them as well as involving them in solving challenges you face.

Making Firing Decisions as a Family Business

Of course, no matter how hard we try, we all make mistakes or face unexpected situations. These mistakes and unexpected outcomes also appear in the hiring decisions we make. Things change all the time too, and we can never be sure that everything we plan and intend will always work out well. So, when we realize that things are not working out with some of our employees, how can we deal with this in a great way?

Again, we come back to the concept of a family business. If you were running a family business and one of the family members was not performing well in the business, what would you do?

Well, it's for sure you wouldn't just 'terminate' them. More than likely, you'd try to find them a more suitable job. Alternatively, if the person actually has something else they want to do outside of the company, you can consider letting the person move on to a new external opportunity.

The idea is not that complicated. If you care about someone enough, you will always find the best solution for the person. No one likes to work without feeling that they are adding value or without feeling appreciated and valued. So with caring as the core value, firing or re-positioning is not a negative thing for the business to do. It is a constructive, reasonable and caring decision the company makes along with the employee.

But if employers do not fundamentally trust their employees and if they see employment negotiations as 'who gets more' strategic negotiations, they will feel insecure or hostile about the discussions they have. And that's especially true in some countries where employment regulations are seen as (and often are) favoring the employees over employers.

You might hear about businesses being sued by their employees or being 'bashed' by the media for mistreating their employees. Fortunately, these stories will not affect your business if you've simply formed a concrete sense of trust and caring with your team.

This sense of trust can only be established when you see all your team members and stakeholders as an integral part of your business. It's easy to do so when you see your business as a Family Business.

IDENTIFYING YOUR VALUES IN YOUR GIVING BUSINESS

Your Mission

Most businesses these days have written mission statements.

After all, most management books say that it's critical to have one. And if you've ever created a business plan, it's a key element you normally indicate right at the beginning of the document.

So let's look at the mission statements of some well-known companies from different industries. These are what we can find online today.

Google

Google's mission is to organize the world's information and make it universally accessible and useful.[14]

Apple

Apple designs Macs, the best personal computers in the world, along with OS X, iLife, iWork and professional software. Apple leads the digital music revolution with its iPods and iTunes online store. Apple has reinvented the mobile phone with its revolutionary iPhone and App store, and is defining the future of mobile media and computing devices with iPad.[15]

McDonald's

Our purpose goes beyond what we sell. We're using our reach to be a positive force. For our customers. Our people. Our communities. Our world.[16]

IKEA

At IKEA our vision is to create a better everyday life for many people. Our business idea supports this vision by offering a wide range of well-designed, functional home furnishing products at prices so low that as many people as possible will be able to afford them.[17]

American Express

At American Express®, we have a mission to be the world's most respected service brand. To do this, we have established a culture that supports our team members, so they can provide exceptional services to our customers.[18]

Patagonia

To build the best product, to cause no unnecessary harm, to use business to inspire and implement solutions to the environmental crisis. For us at Patagonia, a love of wild and beautiful places demands participation in the fight to save them, and to help reverse the steep decline in the overall environmental health of our planet.[19]

Unilever

Our purpose is to make sustainable living commonplace. We work to create a better future every day, with brands and services that help people feel good, look good, and get more out of life.[20]

Comparing the examples on this list, you might have found that Apple's mission statement (the one we currently find by Googling) is quite dull compared to the others, regardless of the fact that Apple is one of the most valued brands today.

This is because this particular mission statement is focused on their products and not on their purpose and mission. Contrast it with some of the statements and quotes by Steve Jobs during the earlier years of Apple.

> *"To make a contribution to the world by making tools for the mind that advance humankind."*

> *"Here's to the crazy ones, the misfits, the rebels, the troublemakers, the round pegs in the square holes... The ones who see things differently—they're not fond of rules... You can quote them, disagree with them, glorify or vilify them, but the only thing you can't do is ignore them because they change things... They push the human race forward, and while some may see them as the crazy ones, we see genius, because the ones who are crazy enough to think that they can change the world, are the ones who do."*

> *"I think part of what made the Macintosh great was that the people working on it were musicians and poets and artists and zoologists and historians who also happened to be the best computer scientists in the world."*

Now, you can see the origins of Apple and how its direction and product design were formulated, enabling it to become the influential company that it is today.

If you were a very talented and motivated individual looking for a great company to work for, which statement would you be attracted to? Is your company's mission statement more about describing what you do? Or does it represent the greater vision of your business and the values you stand for in a way that resonates with the right people?

18 Minutes to Transform Your Business

In late 2009, a then unknown writer took to the TEDx stage.

The 18-minute speech (TED speeches are limited to 18 minutes) Simon Sinek delivered that day has been viewed more than 25 million times. (and it has impacted countless more lives).

In his best-selling book, '*Start with WHY*', he explores how leaders can inspire cooperation, trust and change.[21] He re-defines the power of communicating purpose, putting it simply like this: "*People don't buy what you do; they buy why you do it.*"

He also describes the importance of clarifying your WHY not just in what you communicate, but in what you do every day, "*All organizations start with WHY, but only the great ones keep their WHY clear year after year. Those who forget WHY they were founded show up to the race every day to outdo someone else instead of to outdo themselves. The pursuit, for those who lose sight of WHY they are running the race, is for the medal or to beat someone else.*"

Your mission, regarded as your WHY, has a greater impact on the development of your business than many other aspects of your business combined if you want to maximize the positive impact your business creates.

In a later work, Simon Sinek puts it this way: "*Differentiation comes from clarity of WHY, not excess of WHAT.*"

He talks about how so many people think that adding more *things*, more features, more variety, more choices, makes what they do more compelling and special. But it can be just the opposite. You can be more attractive by having less, but with more meaning.

Clarifying your WHY right at the beginning of your venture is crucial, because filling in the details around these statements gets you headed on the right track; *"I'm in business to…,"* *"I get up in the morning to…,"* or *"we do what we do at our company because…"*

Your why is not *"to make money"* because there must be a reason you want to make money. If a business only exists to make money, it attracts people who are also there to simply earn money in exchange for their time. The real reason for any business to make money is to deliver greater value, solve specific problems or create something that matters.

When you are clear on your WHY, and you can articulate it clearly to yourself, to your team, to your customers, and to the greater world, you attract the people who choose to do business with you because they believe in your WHY, and they will stay with you through good and bad times.

Finally, your WHY should be about **giving**. It should be about you giving something; tangible value, improved lives, connected moments, inspiration and dreams. It shouldn't be about you getting something.

The Ownership of WHY

Having clarity on your WHY gives you direction. You can see and feel where you're heading, and that impacts you, those around you and your customers each and every day.

However, having everyone on the team move in-sync requires more than having a clear direction and destination. It requires every team member to know how to deal with everyday challenges and make the right decisions that contribute to the long-term progress of the company.

Equally, just giving detailed instructions to everyone to increase productivity or to avoid problems does not necessarily help you achieve something greater than what ordinary businesses are doing.

When you have too many rules and instructions, people become afraid of making their own decisions and become afraid of breaking rules. When these employees face situations that are not in the rulebook, they can feel lost. They wouldn't know what to do other than to pass the case to their supervisors. This answers why many business owners still wonder why their employees are never willing to do more than expected (or demanded) or why their people never take on more responsibility.

To become a *leading* organization, you need people who can lead, people who can make their own decisions and act as an integral part of your business, thinking and acting within the spirit of the company's WHY. They need to have the ability to work and act with *ownership thinking*.

In his book, '*What You Really Need to Lead*', Robert Steven Kaplan, a leadership expert, professor and Senior Associate Dean at Harvard Business School, challenges the conventional thinking around the term leadership. He puts it like this, *"Leadership isn't reserved for presidents, generals, and CEOs—the 'big shots'. You don't need a written invitation to be a leader. It is a mindset and way of behavior that begins today."*[22]

Kaplan believes that learning to lead involves three key elements:

1. *Thinking like an owner*

2. *Willingness to act on your beliefs*

3. *Relentless focus on adding value to others*

He argues that great organizations are built around a nucleus of people who think and act with an ownership mindset. He believes that leadership is not a role reserved only for those blessed with the right attributes or situated in the right position of power. *"Leadership,"* says Kaplan, *"is accessible to each of us."*

It means that any of your team members can and should learn to become a leader in his or her own way for the company to succeed. And the role of those leaders should be to create an environment where this change can easily take place. It starts with you clearly communicating your WHY, setting the best example, telling stories that inspire, listening and empowering others on the team and instilling a real sense of ownership in everyone.

When you have your clear WHY and a great 'ownership-taking' team, the members follow your example and even do greater things than what you can do alone.

The Power of Memorable Values

For you to play the game fully, you and your team need to understand the rules of the game and have a set of useful guidelines. These rules and directives do not exist to constrain or micromanage the players of the game. They exist to enhance the effectiveness and enjoyment of the game.

If you play sports, you know that having a good coach and useful guidance and encouragement helps you to become a better player. And you need great teamwork to be truly successful. You even need good competitors to continue improving yourself. You can't just become a better player by practicing alone day after day with no guidance, support or encouragement.

In business too, having experienced coaches and clear guidelines helps the growth of the team players. When the team gets bigger and bigger, having a clear structure helps new team members understand the game and helps them contribute positively to the team's dynamics.

Of course, those who are not the right match will leave quickly too because they see the clear reasons why it is not a good fit for them.

And if a company loses track of what is happening in the first few days, weeks and months of the newest employees joining them, they are likely to get painful surprises later on. The talents you invested a lot of time and money to find might leave because they don't feel inspired. And sadly for you, perhaps, those who are not adding value might continue to stay because there are no reasons for them to leave.

So, before getting into that kind of challenge, you can map out your values clearly and involve everyone on the team to identify with those values. It's important that these values are not just coming from you but from your entire (current) team, so the words you choose are the ones that resonate with your team too.

You don't need to worry about having everything mapped out from the beginning because you can always tweak the language of your values as you go along if you find more important elements later to achieve your shared goal.

In our company, we have created a set of core values with the acronym, '**DO CARE**'.

Desire to improve

Open-mindedness

Courage

Accountability

Respect

Enjoyment

We believe that **doing** and **caring** together create significant outcomes;

positive impacts. Great ideas without actions or many actions without clear intention do not create the real results we desire.

This acronym emerged accidentally when we were asking our team members to list out all the values they thought we had to embrace individually, and together as a team.

After jotting down all the words (we had at least 60), we combined the similar items, crossed out the ones that are nice to have but not critical for everyone. We are all different, so we don't need to try and attain **all** of the positive qualities that are desirable. Some people are naturally superior at certain things, so the entire team can leverage on each other's strengths rather than trying to make everyone perfect at everything. And when we continued to cross out more words, we realized that certain items were remaining on the list that we felt every one of us must have to achieve our objectives together.

Remembering and Reviewing

Clear company values are great to have.

Having excellent clarity around your key values helps all of your team members act with more confidence. That set of values also inspires them to grow their qualities as individual contributors. However, clearly stating the values alone might not really transform or benefit the culture of your business. These values are to be **used** all the time in your business to create the greater outcome you (and your family) want.

Also, when you have words alone, your team might think they already have the qualities those words embody without them really showing up in their actual behaviors. For example, does having a key value like 'Desire to improve' actually mean that people feel they want to improve things? We've found that adding a very clear meaning to each of the words makes a big difference. And there's another crucial part too. But first, here's what we have done.

Desire to improve	Each time, improve something.
Open-mindedness	Be open to new ideas and change.
Courage	Tackle difficult tasks. Stay integral.
Accountability	Deliver on promises with no excuses.
Respect	Find best solutions with respect for others.
Enjoyment	Find ways to enjoy every task.

Now, it's clearer, isn't it?

But the real secret is this: we discuss these points each morning in our team get-together. Through this ritual, we continue to refine and re-evaluate what these values mean and how what we do can be improved in very specific ways. Here's how it works.

We have a daily morning team meeting starting at 9:50 am. And this brief catch-up begins with 2-3 minutes of sharing by one of our team members. They can share insights and ideas; usually something that relates to one of our DO CARE values. For example, someone might say, "*I had such and such experience over the weekend and thought it was an excellent example of Open-mindedness.*" After this, the remaining team members mention what they are focused on achieving for the day.

This way, our morning always starts with inspiration and aspiration coming from the team. And since we began this morning ritual, every member of our team became very familiar with the company values. Now we all pay more attention to what is happening in our workplace and how we can improve what we do.

Taking 10-15 minutes of everyone's time daily might seem wasteful. However, once you see the value of bringing the team together this way, you will no longer want your team to just be doing their jobs without understanding how the entire team is working together to produce the right outcome. If you have a much bigger team, you can do something like this by grouping people into smaller project teams.

We also do quarterly team reviews with each team member. We dig deeper into their performance, personal goals and results using the DO CARE values with a strong focus on self-evaluation. Before the quarterly reviews, each team member works on evaluating themselves on each of the value elements (on a scale of 1-10) and identifies the reason for the rating, and what can be done to improve it further.

When we do this self-evaluation, new team members tend to evaluate themselves quite equally on all items. And this may be because they think that they are doing relatively ok on all points but they do not really see how to improve. So the reviewer (not necessarily a 'boss') can help the person see specific points they can improve upon.

Sometimes, it's useful to ask the person to think of a role model for the quality and think of the particular things this role model actually does.

When we see the specific actions and behaviors our role models demonstrate, we know what we can *do* ourselves to reach our best as well. The key is to let everyone identify clear, actionable improvements they personally commit to make for their own self-improvement.

Positive or Negative Feedback?

It's well known that most people respond better to positive feedback than to negative feedback.

However, it turns out that negative feedback can work well in certain situations. Research by Stacey Finkelstein (Columbia University), Tal Eyal (Ben Gurion University) and Ayelet Fishbach (University of Chicago) sheds light on the seemingly paradoxical nature of feedback, by making it clear why, when, and for whom negative feedback is appropriate.[23]

First, their study clarified the function that positive and negative feedback serve. Positive feedback (e.g., *"Here's what you did really well…"*) increases commitment to the work people do, by enhancing both their experience and their confidence. On the other hand, negative feedback (e.g., *"Here's where you went wrong…"*) is informative; it tells people where they need to spend their effort, and offers insight into how they might improve.

Second, they summed up the consistent outcomes they found from the variety of studies they conducted; ***novices*** *(people with less experience and knowledge)* ***sought and responded well to positive feedback*** *and* ***experts*** *(people with high level of experience and knowledge)* ***sought and responded well to negative feedback***.

Third, they found that both types of feedback could be more effective when they are **constructive.** To give feedback that produces better outcomes, positive information provided should not be needlessly flattering, and negative information shared should not be unnecessarily detrimental.

So this means that when you are working with new team members, it is better to focus more on giving positive encouragement along the way to boost motivation and confidence. And once people become great on the job and form a sense of confidence, we can empower them to see more about how they can improve their qualities and understanding. And in both situations of giving positive and negative feedback, it is better to be more factual and constructive in our feedback and suggestions.

Praising Effort Vs. Talent

Another piece of research conducted by Claudia Mueller and Carol Dweck, expert researchers at Columbia University, offers interesting and instructive insight. They studied 412 fifth graders, ages 10 through 12, comparing the goals and achievements of children praised for their intelligence with those who were commended for making an effort.[24]

The overall findings were that the children who were praised for their effort excelled in making further achievements and those who were told that they were smart were vulnerable to setbacks. *"Praising children's intelligence, far from boosting their self-esteem, encourages them to embrace self-defeating behaviors such as worrying about failure and avoiding risks,"* said Dweck, lead author of the study. *"However, when children are taught the value of concentrating, strategizing and working hard when dealing with academic challenges, this encourages them to sustain their motivation, performance, and self-esteem."*

Let's assume that this finding is also relevant to adult behaviors. This would then mean that creating a culture to acknowledge the effort and improvement made by team members as opposed to a culture of praising and rewarding existing talent and ability helps you create a high-performance environment. It also means that team members will not be afraid of trying new things. They are more likely to innovate. They are not scared of making mistakes to get better.

The lesson here is about finding your *own* WHY and creating the right culture around it so that people really know how to behave as a part of the company identity.

When this is done, your focus on business development becomes straightforward. You can simply concentrate on giving more. And as you're about to discover, that's the best part of being in business.

GIVING MORE AT EVERY STEP

The Real Reason to Be in Business

Businesses exist to create great value.

Whether your business is profit-driven or meaning-driven, the reason that your business exists in the marketplace is to create value you believe in.

And creating value for others is a form of giving.

Now that doesn't mean you need to give things away for free. It means you give more value than what you are paid for.

When your business is highly appreciated for the value you offer, you are likely to succeed. Being highly appreciated by those you serve makes your business more meaningful too.

So, what is the best way to maximize the value we add?

The Value Creation Process

Paul Dunn, my colleague and personal mentor (and coincidentally my husband today), is a respected individual in the small to medium scale business world, particularly in the accounting profession. And rest assured, he's not an Accountant.

Yet he earned the '*Inaugural Outstanding Contribution to the Accounting Profession Award*' in the UK in 2015 for the decades of work he did to bring a new perspective to the role accountants play in the business world.

Starting as one of the first 10 people to work for early business technology company Hewlett Packard (HP) in Australia, he went on to co-create one of Australia's first computer companies, Hartley Computer, and then moved on to consult and empower accountants globally. Together with Ron Baker, he authored the breakthrough business book for the profession, '*The Firm of the Future*'.[25]

Back then, business to him was very simple; by maximizing the value you add through the real connections you form, anyone can grow successful and valued businesses.

He had come up with models and concepts to show people how to do this simply. Borrowing one of these models, we can see that business— any business—can be broken down into a range of processes that flow in a particular sequence.

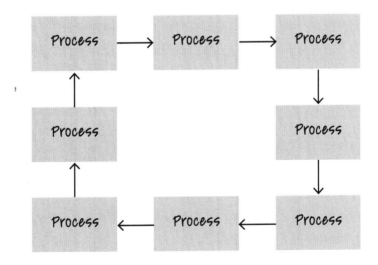

For a restaurant, this process might begin when a customer calls in to make a reservation. And after this, the customer arrives at the restaurant and is taken to a table. And eventually, the food is served and eaten, and then the customer settles the bill. When the transaction is over, it might be seen as the end of the process, but some businesses might have more steps that follow. They might encourage the customer to become a member of their loyalty program or even ask for the customer's birthday to send out a special gift during the birthday month.

Any business can do this 'breaking down' exercise to see how many tiny, often-missed steps (or opportunities for what Paul calls 'connected moments') they have in their business.

And according to Paul, creating a great business is almost entirely about adding extra value and enhanced 'moments of connection' to each of these processes, reviewing what happened and improving them for the next round of opportunities.

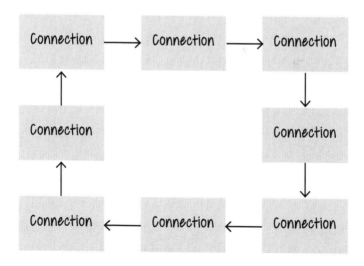

It sounded like an absurdly simple concept to introduce to accountants who were used to the complex analysis and planning. However, in the 'sea of sameness' (where most businesses were behaving like each other), adding greater value, creating a greater sense of connection and enhancing the experience of each and every customer by questioning, innovating, testing and improving made a significant difference. And people were indeed inspired into action by the fresh perspective that Paul brought to their firms.

This method can be applied to many other processes too. We can take a marketing campaign, break it down into small processes and enhance the connection and engagement of each process through each cycle of communication and vice versa. This exercise can also be done independently in different departments in a larger company.

To Paul, seeing many businesses achieve great things by implementing these newly adopted actions was exciting. Every day, there was something new to be discovered and implemented. Business to him was a vehicle of fun, excitement and free expression.

In Search of Meaning

On the other hand, in my earlier life (before I became a business owner), business seemed to me like a 'dark evil force'.

In my early twenties, I traveled around the world as a backpacker. Living and working in many different countries and seeing the overwhelming inequalities in the world, I felt that consumerism and materialism were to be blamed for the lack of real happiness in our world. So at one point, I tried to create my own 'self-sufficient' life by living in a remote rural area of Japan, thinking that "*the key to creating the perfect life is to buy nothing.*" I also thought that if I didn't buy anything, I wouldn't damage anything (i.e. nature).

And I did try. For two years, I learned the art of simple country living and organic farming in a small, tightly knit community, four hours drive away from my hometown.

In the end though, I couldn't create the self-sufficient life I envisioned. The reality was that I still had to buy things occasionally. I still drove a car and often used tools and resources that had been produced by others. And instead of learning about how to create an entirely self-sufficient life, I started to see the underlying connectedness of the world and how I was merely a small part of something bigger.

One of the best things I learned living the rural life was the wisdom of local farmers about co-existing with nature; cultivating the abundance working with and not against the natural cycles, and always taking care of the land no matter how much extra work it required.

Growing my own food and living with nature, and minimizing the use of external resources was hard work. We even had to scoop up our own 'waste' from the toilet regularly. But my life was full of joyful moments, sharing whatever I had with others in the community.

Everyone shared what he or she had, and we helped each other whenever someone needed help. And I started to care less and less about self-sufficiency altogether. I became aware that others always supported me; my friends in the farming community, my family back home, and people who were producing the things I occasionally bought to solve my problems or to fulfill my needs. I failed to disconnect my life entirely from the world outside. And I eventually saw that it was not necessary to disconnect at all.

I was initially embarrassed, realizing how judgmental I had been. After all, I admitted, we were all the same; we were all trying to create a better life, a better future. We all cared for our own friends, families and children. No single person was to be blamed directly for the environmental and social issues that were created through our lifestyle and business activities. I was no better than anyone else, and creating a self-sufficient life meant very little other than my selfish idea—one of wanting to be *right*.

Subsequently, I went out again into the world. And this time, I started looking for clues to a better way. I still believed that there were some things I was not seeing. Because it still didn't make sense to me that there were so many people who had so little while so many others were not feeling fulfilled even though they had so much more.

And then it dawned on me: I wondered *"what if businesses were to become the real change-makers in our world."*

I couldn't see anything else as powerful as the businesses that were actually driving the direction of the world and connecting people beyond all their cultural, racial and religious differences.

In the Middle of Polarities...

When Paul 'retired' in 2000, he was initially quite happy pottering around in Southern France. But being the kind of person who cannot sit around for too long, he came back to the business world in 2005.

He realized that being retired and doing the things he imagined he wanted to do didn't keep him content for long. He realized that being innovative and productive mattered so much more than having a nice relaxing retirement.

When I met Paul in 2006 in Australia, I was a mother of two young kids with a small and demanding food business trying to find a way to solve some of the world's social problems in a small way (you'll see more on this in the next chapter). Paul simply wanted to do something great again in business. So we were looking for different things. But what we both knew was the potential power of businesses to create real change.

And that was when we first came up with the idea of Buy1GIVE1 (B1G1). A simple idea that we saw could harness the power of business in a new and powerful way. We believed that businesses with a real sense of purpose and caring could transform our world, and we wanted to empower them to do so.

Creating More Meaning Through Empathy

I said earlier that the power of business is in the value it produces. And the greatest value is often derived from caring and empathy. Empathy is the capacity to understand or feel what another person is experiencing from within that person's frame of reference, i.e., the ability to place yourself in someone else's position.

A business with empathy is a business with wisdom. An empathetic business can feel the pains its customers are feeling and come up with the best solutions to help them solve those issues.

In her best-selling book, '*Meaningful*', Bernadette Jiwa, one of the most influential business bloggers and brand consultants in Australia, expresses it like this:

> "*The best products and services in the world don't simply invite people to say 'this is awesome'; they remind people of how great they are themselves.*
>
> *People are choosing to spend their money with companies whose actions resonate with their values—companies that thrive by doing the right thing and by making things customers love instead of trying to get customers to love their things.*
>
> *Our job is not simply to obsess about the features and benefits of*

what we're making: it is to wonder and care about the difference
we can make to people and to our world."[26]

Many prosperous businesses have this figured out already. They understand almost intuitively that really understanding their own customers directly leads to increased business. So, having a team with greater capacity to empathize enhances the chance of your company's success as well.

Business With Empathy

Truly empathetic businesses also feel the pains and desires of many others. These 'others' include their own employees and their family members, their suppliers and their contractors. This might even include the lives of people living in the countries that they import their resources from or those who are suffering in the world at large. While taking care of these 'others' might not offer any financial returns directly to the business, truly empathetic businesses would still try to do what they can to create a better life for those around them. And some of them manage to create an empathetic environment by sharing stories and 'connecting' even more deeply.

If you visit the Starbucks' website (either their global or regional site), you will see this statement;

> **We have always believed Starbucks can—and should—have a positive impact on the communities we serve. One person, one cup and one neighborhood at a time.**[27]

And then they go on to talk about three key areas they regularly engage in: community, ethical sourcing and environment. To engage customers in what they care about, Starbucks often uses beautiful pictures on the wall to tell stories of coffee farmers.

One of our team members at B1G1 used to work at Starbucks when she was a student. And today, she still enthusiastically talks about the experience of working at Starbucks as one of the most valuable earlier life experiences she has had. It has impacted who she is today.

She talks about how Starbucks regarded each member of its staff (or *partners* as Starbucks calls them) as a member of the *family*. And by inspiring and growing their employees to work together with empathy, companies like Starbucks make a continuous effort to improve every part of their business processes and try to connect more deeply with their customers. And Starbucks is definitely not the cheapest place to buy a cup of coffee.

When you create this focus in your business, your value generation exercise chart becomes like this.

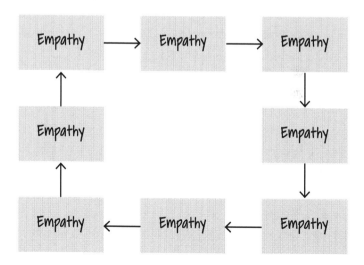

In each process and part of your business, you can use empathy as a tool to create greater meaning and a deeper sense of connection.

Cultivating Empathy in Your Business

In the olden days, businesses with great empathy were more common because the owners and the decision makers were always present in their businesses and connecting with their customers. They understood the importance of creating trusting relationships with the people in their community. But more importantly, they acted as individuals who cared.

Today it's different. In the move towards globalization, businesses became more compartmentalized with multi-level management structures. Now many tasks are outsourced, so the person facing a customer may not be someone who can make necessary decisions.

When people in business are not given the right to make their own decisions, they tend to act as though they are trying to serve the employer's financial interest above other things. This is usually because that's what people feel they are evaluated on. Some people even prioritize their own needs and convenience above the needs of their customers. This model is part of the reason for the degradation of trust surrounding businesses today.

After observing this issue, many large companies started to implement training programs to increase the level of customer service or set up their own CSR departments to strategize how to become more socially responsible. But this approach alone has a limitation; personal traits like empathy cannot just be created through ad-hoc training programs or plugged into the culture as a strategic add-on. It has to be part of the identity of the organizations from the core; it has to come from the genuine caring of the founders, directors, managers and employees. When a business creates an empathetic culture, it develops the greatest capacity to innovate and creates real value for its customers too.

Forming an empathetic culture is an ongoing process. To really cultivate an empathetic culture, you need to become the one to care. What you think, do, write, discuss; all these things play a part in embedding real empathy in your workplace. If you are consciously listening, understanding, helping and encouraging, people around you and the team you lead will follow your example.

But if you are the one who complains, talks negatively about others behind their backs or jumps on to negative judgment without understanding the situation fully, you will create a culture of judgment and cynicism. And no matter how hard you try to hide it, it will be evident to everyone around you.

Bringing back empathy in business is no longer just a nice thing to do. It's critical. It draws the line between companies that are consumed by the bottom line and companies that have more impact by prioritizing purpose and meaning—those that are inspired to care.

So next, we are going to look into the power of giving to see how giving that is created through empathy can become the winning formula for a thriving life and business.

CHAPTER 3

THE POWER OF GIVING

When I chased after money, I never had enough.

When I got my life on purpose and focused on giving of myself and everything that arrived into my life, then I was prosperous.

Wayne Dyer

GIVING AND GETTING

When you were growing up, people around you probably taught you to become a *go-getter*.

Getting more things seemed to be the quickest way to happiness. And to get more of the things we wanted to have, we had to be more proactive and results-oriented. We had to rise above the competition.

This focus led us to work harder, sometimes even with great sacrifice or against a lot of resistance. We thought that we had to work hard to get more things in our lives to become happy and successful. We worked hard to get more of our parents' attention, to get better grades at school, to get into more prestigious schools, to get more secure and highly paid jobs, to get bigger homes and so on.

Our lives became centered on trying to get more things. Yet the key driver of our desire to have more is actually our desire to simply become happy and fulfilled.

Having more of the same things in bigger, faster, newer or cooler formats might not make us more fulfilled in the long run. And what often follows after an event of getting and having is this: *losing*.

The Getting Cycle

It works like this: the things we have are temporary. Although having many joyful moments in life is important, just having more things might not lead to **long-term** happiness. This is because our appreciation for these things does not last forever.

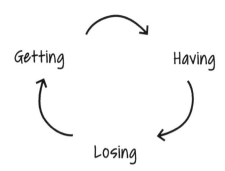

Something you really wanted and managed to get at some point in the past is probably sitting in your storage space forgotten and unwanted now. Many people's houses are so full of things that they even have difficulty getting rid of them.

When we want something, we feel that getting it will make us happy. We want to get it before someone else gets it. We want to get more of it than others. And when we focus on getting more, we cannot help noticing other people who have more, who try to get more, who try to have more than we have.

When we live day-in and day-out in this cycle, there is an underlying feeling that we do not have enough; a feeling of *deficiency*. And we are less likely to feel satisfied in much of our journey, looking for something more.

The Giving Cycle

Now, let's look at another possibility; a different pattern.

In this cycle, we start from the status of *having*, being grateful and appreciating what we have. And because we recognize the fact that we already have what we want, we feel that we have enough and we are happy to give some of the things we have to others. We find joy in seeing others being fulfilled.

We pay more attention to the opportunities to give than to the opportunities to get. And interestingly, when we create a giving tendency around us, we are more likely to **receive** things we want more naturally and effortlessly.

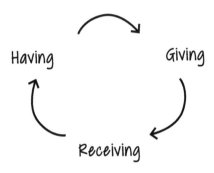

This cycle of giving creates an ongoing sense of sufficiency and gratitude. And when we live in this cycle, we notice and attract people who are also givers. They pay attention to more opportunities to give. Subsequently, the cycle perpetuates and grows, and as a result, we feel more content, more grateful and more generous.

Just think of it: do you think it's easier to be loved when you are trying to be loved or when you are being loving to others? Do you think it's easier to **feel** wealthy when you are trying to get more money or when you are appreciating and sharing what you already have?

We can stop wishing that others behaved differently or that the world worked differently. Because the world works differently only if the game's main player (yes, it's you) can play the game differently.

Mahatma Gandhi said, "*Be the change you want to see in the world.*"

Changing the game you play takes only a moment. You can choose to create more giving tendencies around you. Right now.

All you need is a shift in **your** perception. Just like that. It couldn't be any easier.

BUYING HAPPINESS

In a Harvard Study published in 2014 titled '*Spending and Happiness: Using Money to Benefit Others Pays Off*', researchers Elizabeth Dunn, Lara Aknin and Michael Norton conducted various experiments and found out that spending money on others (termed '*prosocial spending*') boosts people's emotional and physical well-being.[28]

The Happiness Study

Their experiment began in 2008 when they gave a sum of money (ranging from $5 to $20) to random people on a university campus. They asked half of these people to spend it on themselves and the other half to spend it on someone else.

At the end of the day, they observed that people who spent the money on someone else generally reported feeling happier.

That finding led them to conduct further research to verify and explore the benefit of spending money on others. Their research spanned different socio-economic classes, races and age groups.

Then in a 2012 study, they conducted a test with young children. They gave each child a pile of treats and observed how their facial expressions (happiness level) changed when they are directly given treats themselves and when they are given the opportunity to offer a treat to a puppet.

And in fact, happiness of the children peaked when they offered a treat from *their own pile* of treats instead of just giving a treat they did not own.

While these findings suggest that we all share the natural human tendency to experience joy in benefiting others, Dunn, Aknin and Norton also tell us that not all forms of pro-social spending produce emotional benefits.

They say that the greatest emotional benefits of giving, or pro-social spending, are seen when the givers experience emotional connections with the recipients of their gifts; for example when they could see the *impact* of their gifts and when they are given a choice to give (rather than being forced to give). So given the right conditions, this research means that we are more likely to feel happier when we are giving and sharing than when we are experiencing our own gain.

There are also medical studies that identify the increased release of brain chemicals like serotonin, endorphins, and dopamine when we perform an act of giving. These chemicals are associated with improved moods and feelings of increased well-being. Having more of these chemicals in our system makes us feel happy (and they even help us become healthier).

100 Percent Chance of Happiness...?

These discoveries conflict with some of our common ideas. Ideas like what TV commercials often tell us—that we can become better and happier when we get more things, better things, for ourselves. Credit cards allow us to buy things even when we don't have the money to buy them. Some people sacrifice their relationships and health to gain greater financial wealth or fame.

But just having more things doesn't make people happier for too long. That's because what we are really seeking is the feeling of fulfillment.

If you think that it's unfair that some people have much more than you, the grass is (and will be) always greener on the other side of the fence. When we compare ourselves with those who have more than us, we are less likely to be satisfied with our own lives.

On the other hand, if we compare ourselves with those who seem to have less or those who have greater challenges than we do, we are more likely to feel grateful for what we have and feel more generous to share what we have with those who have less.

The great news is that **giving is actually easier than getting**.

Giving starts with the things we have. If we already have something and if we think that we have enough, then we can choose to give and share it.

Getting, on the other hand, starts with what we don't have. Getting what we want isn't always within our control. The outcome depends on others or external conditions too. So, the chance of us getting what we want is never 100 percent no matter how hard we try, while the chance of giving what we have is always 100 percent as long as we choose to do it.

How great is it that we can all experience more happiness this way? It means that we will feel more fulfilled just by incorporating more of this giving focus.

We no longer need to complain that life is not fair or that we don't have enough. Because no matter how little we have, we can always find a way to share a part of what we have. And as a result, we can experience more abundance in life, in our relationships and in business.

Let's start doing more pro-social spending: giving and sharing all the gifts we have.

THE CONSEQUENCES OF OUR GIVING

Even though we now see giving as the key to happiness and abundance, we also need to know that there are negative consequences that our giving can create. And that happens when it's done in the *wrong* way. Here is one common mistake.

Giving Reluctantly

Frequently, when people give, there is a reluctance about doing it. For example, a mother giving a treat to a child to stop the child throwing a tantrum. This way of 'giving' only encourages the child to throw more tantrums later.

A person lending money to a friend with a financial problem just because he was asked and was too uncomfortable to decline would often experience more awkward situations afterwards (like having to ask for the repayment and eventually feeling let down in the relationship).

Making a donation because someone from a charity knocked on your door and asked for it persistently could lead you to develop a sense of distrust and skepticism about giving to charities as a whole.

What's happening here are examples of how some forms of giving can create undesired outcomes if we give reluctantly in certain situations, usually through guilt.

Let's take a deeper look at what's happening.

When you want something that someone else has, there are two main ways for you to obtain it.

One approach is just to ask for it and persist until you get it. Another method is to offer something else with a higher (perceived) value in exchange so that the other person would naturally want to give it to you.

In childhood, it's often possible to get away with the first approach. You see it frequently when a child cries loudly and mum comes running.

When children get tired, most of them will persistently ask to be carried and eventually manage to make adults pick them up.

But imagine a place where everyone is always asking others to give away more things without offering any value in return. It doesn't seem to be a nice place to be, even if our requests are met in the end through persistence and persuasion.

That's why some charity giving can create negative feelings. When you give reluctantly to someone who is 'begging', it could encourage the person to keep begging. And that can potentially compromise the individual's self-esteem, productivity and independence while reducing your joy of giving too.

If the beneficiaries of your charitable contributions perceive that someone *rich* helped them because they were pitied for being poor or disadvantaged, they could establish a sense of dependency and feeling of entitlement to continue being on the receiving end too.

Balanced Giving

Happier relationships and communities are built on fair value exchanges. Companies that generously acknowledge the great effort made by their employees attract more talent, productivity and increased business.

Charities that raise the self-esteem of people they help maximize the positive impact they create long-term rather than just giving out aid and perceiving beneficiaries as the 'needy' ones.

And in these situations, people (on both the giving and receiving ends) are more likely to become happier because they all end up becoming the *givers*.

It's important to remember that everyone can offer value, even if it is not monetary or conventional value.

Even in a close relationship or in a love affair, we need to be able to exchange value. We are trading every day in this game of life. And becoming a great *trader*—a giver of great value—makes us a better game player. When all of us are exchanging great value all the time, we have more fun and have meaningful experiences in this game together.

So, let's summarize it like this. The better way of giving is to give:

↗   *when you see value in the exchange*

↗   *when you feel great about it*

↗   *when you feel it's the right thing to do*

↗   *when you want to help someone to experience a greater life*

When your giving doesn't fit any of these conditions (such as *when you feel guilty to turn down a request*), you can say 'no' to the opportunity even if you feel uncomfortable to decline it initially.

It's also helpful to explain to the other party why you are not doing the things you were asked to do. You can do so with care and respect. Maybe you can offer something else that you think is more beneficial to the person and the situation. Consciously giving and receiving helps everyone to play the game fully and have the maximum enjoyment.

And once you stop giving reluctantly and start giving more happily, you stop seeing the negative consequences.

Giving With Expectations

Even though we are always exchanging value, by far the best way to give is not to have fixed expectations.

If you feel upset when the person you helped didn't thank you or if your giving didn't create the outcome you wanted to create, then your own joy and fulfillment through the giving is lessened. For example, if you expect your children to appreciate you for the hard work you do to raise them, you're likely to be disappointed when they don't express as much appreciation as you think they should.

This is different from parents teaching their children to appreciate and thank people appropriately. Rather than trying to be appreciated themselves, these parents are only passing on a habit of gratitude to their children so that they can become better game-players in the game of life.

Having the ability to appreciate definitely makes our game far more enjoyable. However, appreciation shouldn't be expected because having expectations diminishes the pure joy of giving. When our giving has *strings* attached, we are likely to be disappointed later.

Giving is supposed to make **us** feel happy. We are doing it for ourselves. It's a selfish act. Helping someone else or sharing what we have enhances our own life experiences. It helps us feel more contented, and it even helps us become healthier. It means we don't need to be thanked for what we do. If anything, we should really be the ones to thank others for the opportunities they are giving us.

With this perspective, it's almost impossible to become dissatisfied with your giving. And you'll be surprised that you actually end up receiving even more appreciation when you don't expect it.

CHARITIES, SOCIAL BUSINESSES AND EFFECTIVE GIVING

When we use the word 'giving', many people think of charities. In fact, when you perform a Google search on that word, the majority of search results are about charity giving.

Search engines are, of course, among the most powerful marketing tools for businesses these days. And even for charity organizations, it is no exception. They want to own the giving space. They are, indeed, in the *business of giving*.

Yet, most interestingly (and more and more frequently too), the word '*charity*' has some negative connotations. Here are some of the perceptions around charities and parallel ideas about businesses.

Idea 1-a: "We cannot trust charities these days."
We have all seen news about significant charity scandals. Many people think that it is hard to trust charity organizations nowadays. One big charity scandal can negatively impact the entire charity giving space for a long time.

Idea 1-b: "Some businesses have broken promises. But we should give them a second chance."
We have also seen news about businesses that have broken rules, fudged numbers or lied to consumers. But we react differently. With businesses, we are more likely to accept the fact that the misconduct was carried out by specific individuals and not by

everyone in the business. And even more interestingly, some of the corporations who broke the rules, fudged the numbers or lied to the customers were even bailed out by their governments.

These are fascinating contradictions. Although the devastation caused by broken promises made by businesses are potentially far greater, we tend to get more disillusioned by the misconduct of charity organizations.

When large companies break their promises, it can potentially damage our environment and health, create financial havoc or even cause life-threatening conditions. It actually can have a more direct impact on our own lives. However, when we hear of a business breaking promises, it doesn't ring the same kind of alarm bells as when we hear of charities breaking the promises they've made.

It is perhaps because businesses are seen to be the providers of value rather than the recipients of our goodwill.

Idea 2-a: "Charities should have no admin cost."
Because of news reports we've seen about excessive salaries paid to top executives (plus extremely high administrative and fundraising cost percentages) of some well-known charity organizations, the public has started to think that charities should not have administrative costs.

Idea 2-b: "Businesses should invest in scalability."
On the other hand, businesses are expected to invest in sales and marketing, intellectual property, system development and a skilled workforce. While it's important to be cost effective in business too, capability building activities are highly valued in business.

Again, this comparison shows that we often expect businesses and charities to have very different approaches. While we accept that businesses need to invest in their growth, we often do not empower charity organizations to focus on the same. And this perception can lead to many challenges and limitations in the charity world.

Many charity organizations find it hard to employ skilled workers or to invest in capacity and capability building activities because they are expected to keep their costs down to the barest minimum. Yes, we should all try to be as cost effective as possible to achieve our goals. But it doesn't mean that we need to expect charity organizations to always operate with bare minimum resources.

Idea 3-a: "Charities = Recipients"

We think that charities are here to receive donations from people because they are doing good things. The charities themselves might think that too. But why is it that we don't really think of charities as providers of value? They give us opportunities to feel great by allowing us to give what we can give; they are selling *happiness* in that way— and, at the same time, they deliver significant benefits to people, the kind of 'feel-good' experience you cannot normally buy.

Idea 3-b: "Businesses = Making Money"

We automatically think that the primary objective of businesses is to make money. But is it true? Can't businesses have different objectives? And isn't money simply a tool for them to do more of whatever they aspire to do? If the objective of business is to do some good to benefit people, isn't it trying to do the same thing as a charity?

The type of expectations we have for the objectives of businesses and charities may also be dividing what these entities generally focus on.

If charities focused more on delivering value, their sustainability issues might be solved. And if businesses are encouraged to work on creating a positive impact, they might make decisions in very different ways too.

These ideas here are just a starting point for us to consider that charities and businesses can be treated in the same way, or at least, they can be encouraged to work towards coming closer together.

It's an interesting idea to consider. It opens up our minds to many new possibilities.

Emerging Social Businesses

The term 'Social Enterprise' has become much more widely known in recent years. And there are many variations of its definition.

To describe the concept, I tend to use the term 'Social Business'. It's a term clearly defined by Nobel Peace Prize Laureate Prof. Muhammad Yunus.[29]

In his book 'Creating a world without poverty', Prof. Yunus says that a Social Business is:

↗ *created and designed to address a social problem*

↗ *a non-loss, non-dividend company, i.e.*

- *it is financially self-sustainable and*
- *profits realized by the business are reinvested in the business itself (or used to start other social businesses), with the aim of increasing social impact; for example expanding the company's reach, improving the products or services or in other ways subsidizing the social mission.*

Unlike a profit-maximizing business model, the prime aim of a Social

Business is not to maximize profits (although you'll note that Prof. Yunus suggests that generating profits is important to increase its social impact).

What makes Social Businesses different from regular businesses is the fact that they **start** with an aim to address social issues. And what makes Social Businesses different from charities is the fact that they are commercially viable (financially self-sustainable—they don't need *donations* to survive and prosper).

By understanding this, you can probably see that if every business in our world started and operated as a Social Business, the world would become a very different place. This is because Social Businesses would make entirely different decisions every day while also being focused on generating value just like any other business.

At the same time, if every charity started and operated more like a Social Business, the world would become a very different place too. And not surprisingly in this meaning-driven world, these transitions are already emerging.

More and more entrepreneurs are starting their businesses with a strong social mission (for example, *Warby Parker, Whole Foods Market* and so on). They are investing their time and effort into something that's much more meaningful than just making money. And more and more charity organizations are starting to work on making the giving experience tangible, and embracing the enterprising spirit to make their activities sustainable (for example, *Charity Water* and *Kiva).*

As fascinating as it seems, we could indeed be heading to a world where there is no boundary between businesses and charities. The emergence of well-supported Social Businesses shows that this trend is gaining momentum.

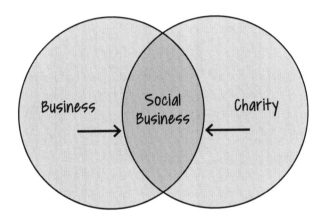

If that were happening at an even faster pace, then maybe most of the problems we currently have could be solved in creative, effective and value-adding ways.

Effective Giving

Now, let's look at the concept of Effective Giving to better understand how to address social problems with greater impact.

People have different ideas about what Effective Giving means. Some say it's about reducing the overhead of the charitable activities or increasing the outcome (the social impact) to create the maximum impact with the smallest amount of investment. Others say it's about integrating community development and capacity building into aid projects so that long-term results can be created in developing nations. And there are still others who suggest that it's about integrating charitable activities into Corporate Social Responsibility (CSR) initiatives that effectively engage the employees of participating corporations.

What everyone is trying to say here seems to be that Effective Giving brings (or should bring) business-minded thinking and charity-minded thinking closer.

For all of the elements of Effective Giving to flourish, businesses should be thinking like Social Businesses and so should charities.

Businesses can become more aware about the negative social impacts they might be creating and then work towards reducing them AND work on generating more positive social impacts, all the while maximizing the value they provide to their direct customers (which is another form of giving).

Charities can think more about creating financial sustainability around their own activities as well as actively engaging with their donors and beneficiaries to create greater understanding and value exchanges wherever they can.

Challenges of a Small Business

Now, let me take you back to the year 2006. As I said earlier, this was when I met Paul Dunn and came up with the idea for the giving initiative Buy1GIVE1 (please see page 66 if you need a refresher).

Back then, I had been running a food production business called *Bouncing Olive* with my ex-partner and great friend, David Anttony, who co-founded the business with me. We were selling organic frozen meals through health food stores and independent supermarket outlets in Australia. It had taken us more than five years to get to the stage of having more than 140 retail stores in three states on our distribution list since we started our business in New Zealand.

We worked hard to grow our business because we wanted to help underprivileged children by providing access to nourishing food and education through the profits we planned to make. Right from the start, the business had a social mission.

This was largely because both David and I traveled around the world when we were younger, and we were often confronted by the poverty we saw in many 'developing countries'. We wanted to do something about it.

Although I did many things in my early twenties, looking for the meaning of life and trying to find answers to the questions I had about our world, I still couldn't make sense of the fact that so many children were still living on the street or living in poverty with little access to basic resources and education. And I didn't know what to do about it.

So, when I became a mother a few years later and felt the deep sense of love I had never felt before, I started to *see* the faces of those children alongside my baby daughter's face. I thought it was important that we did something to help those disadvantaged children because I felt my daughter could have been just like any one of them.

Starting a business to make a difference made sense to us. We planned to set up our charitable foundation to help many children one day when we became *successful.*

But all of those grand ideas never seemed to happen, no matter how hard we worked in our business. The reality of running a growing business was that we had so many day-to-day challenges to deal with, and we could always find ways to spend or invest all the available money back into the business so that we could continue to grow. We had so much to do every day. And we were not making much profit.

We also listened to other business owners and learned about their ideas, hopes and challenges. We realized that so many other business owners were also willing to give back **IF** it was easy enough for them to do so. They just felt like they didn't have the time, extra funds or knowledge, yet.

Buy1GIVE1 (B1G1)

The original idea of Buy1GIVE1 was initiated by a chance remark made by someone in a discussion group while I was presenting *Bouncing Olive's* business model at a conference. Paul was the group 'mentor' at that point. As I spoke enthusiastically about how we aimed to help feed and educate street children in India with the proceeds made from the sales of our frozen meals, I heard a voice of someone saying, "*Ah, that's* ***buy one, give one.***"

We had all heard of 'buy one, get one' as a sales term but we had never heard of 'buy one, give one'. We were utterly stunned by the simplicity of the idea.

So, when I realized the power of that idea, to give one meal for every packaged meal that we sold—and when I found out that it cost as little as USD 25 cents to give a meal to an impoverished child through long-standing charity organizations in India, it suddenly made total sense to me.

I realized that it was not about trying to do (or wishing to do) something enormous and great in some far-off future. It was about doing something small now, today and every day. We no longer needed to wait until we became *successful* to give. With this approach, any and every business could become a Giving Business, immediately.

I imagined…

> *What if every time someone saw a doctor, a person in need received much needed medical support? What if every time someone bought a book, a tree got planted to protect natural*

habitats? What if every time an electronic store sold a TV set, a blind person received a cataract operation to gain sight? What if every time, someone went to a seminar and learned something great, an underprivileged child received a day's access to education...?

I imagined a world full of giving, where everything we did made a difference in a profound and caring way. At that time, I realized that I finally found what I had been looking for.

And in 2007, we launched Buy1GIVE1 (B1G1), a global giving initiative, so that every business in our world could implement the 'buy one, give one' way of giving.

We eventually decided to sell our food business that we had worked hard for to develop in order to grow this marvelous idea. We knew there was no other initiative like Buy1GIVE1. [Little did we know that organizations like *Toms* (and their *one-for-one* model) were starting around that time as well.] I felt that it was our responsibility to do something about it even though we didn't know how to actually make it happen at that time.

It took us almost three years to figure out *how to* make that simple thought a reality. Since there was no other example for us to follow, we had to figure out so many things, like how to select charity organizations/ NGOs to work with, how to measure and deliver impacts, how to deal with administration, how to create systems that made the giving experience seamless, how to convince businesses to give away their hard-earned money, and how to forward 100 percent of contributions to the nominated causes while funding our own work sustainably.

And we wanted to do all of these things as a business; a social enterprise. It was not easy.

Overcoming the Sustainability Issue

We definitely didn't have the right financial model to stay sustainable right off the bat. So, Paul became the initial benefactor. And he started to inspire and convince many other business owners to join this promising yet then unknown 'movement.' There were times we didn't think we could make it.

Nine years later, Buy1GIVE1 is still here and growing. And today, we have a unique business model. Instead of becoming a charity (and be funded by donations), Buy1GIVE1, a Social Enterprise, is financed by a membership program where we provide unique system features, tools, and resources to participating businesses to make their giving effective. We focus on creating value. And this model allows us always to pass on 100 percent of all donations made via our system to our charity partners (those who run the actual giving projects) around the world. This way, we can maximize the impact of giving while ensuring the sustainability and scalability of the initiative itself with transparency and clarity.

We are grateful for the 1,500+ small-to-medium sized businesses from all industries around the world that have chosen to participate in the initiative and make the 'buy one, give one' idea a reality. It's simply remarkable that these small businesses have together created more than 78 million giving impacts through the B1G1 online giving platform.[30]

When we say *giving impacts*, we are not talking about monetary values. Instead, we are talking about the amount of giving measured in a very different way. For example, one impact could be 'one day's access to clean drinking water', 'one library book given', or 'one day's access to education' or 'one tree planted."

They are significant *differences* created through our 700+ carefully selected projects. And for the small businesses we work with, creating these outcomes (the giving impacts) means a tremendous achievement.

And it could not have happened if we all waited for the *success* to come first.

The Learning on the Ground

When you read what I describe as our journey to this point, it may sound like it was relatively straightforward. But in reality, we have experienced so many challenges along the way.

I've listed some of the important lessons we've learned from experiences we had during years of work in the 'giving industry' that have gotten us where we are today. We've found that these insights are critical in making any form of giving sustainable and efficient. They may become useful for your giving endeavors too.

1. *Making continuous small improvements matter*

   Doing one big thing, just once, despite believing it's the best thing, doesn't usually lead to the best outcome. It's critical to be able to make many small mistakes to create continuous improvements at every stage.

   New charitable projects that are too big from the start (even with excellent planning and intention) often fail in the long run because of the lack of opportunities to make small mistakes and small improvements in early stages.

2. *Real difference comes from inside*

   Outsiders (e.g. donors and volunteers) hardly know what's most beneficial for the people in different communities. So, we can listen closely and let the local population and leaders drive the direction of the initiatives through their own aims, mistakes, and lessons as much as possible.

We can assist their efforts to make real change through providing what we can offer such as funding, external insights, knowledge and tools.

3. *The power of humility*

Giving should be done through humble gratitude. We should not perceive people with challenges as less than us nor overly glorify the givers (donors). Giving with pity creates a relationship of dependency and entitlement. Instead, we can see the challenges and problems we have in the world as opportunities to make a difference together.

Giving makes us happy, so we can be thankful.

When we approach social issues with these perspectives, we are much more likely to create long-term solutions AND find joy in the process.

Through our own experiences of running Buy1GIVE1, we have also learned to embrace three important focus points in our model: IMPACT, HABIT, and CONNECTION. And here's why these three aspects really matter to us.

IMPACT

We break down every challenge into small actionable items so that even tiny giving (as little as one cent) can create tangible impact. This way, more people can give, AND we can measure the accumulated results over time, making the giving experience much more meaningful.

HABIT

Giving back should be part of what we do every day (just like bees pollinating flowers) rather than just as an ad-hoc event. We focus on helping businesses create regular giving habits and a great giving culture.

CONNECTION

Acts of giving creates a sense of connection in businesses and communities. Through Buy1GIVE1, we provide tools and resources to enhance that sense of connection you experience at every level. We cannot solve all problems alone, but we can make a significant difference by working together.

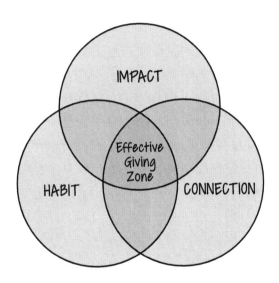

If you ever incorporate giving in your own business or go to work for charitable causes, I hope you can explore your own model of giving carefully so that your effort will create maximum impact too.

Possible Issues of Big Giving

The reason we decided to focus on working with smaller businesses initially rather than large corporations was that we saw the need; we realized that small business owners wanted to make a difference but didn't know how, or didn't have the time and resources to do so. They didn't have a CSR department to figure things out. Nor did they have large amounts of money to give away.

For the same reason, we focused on working with smaller charity organizations rather than trying to recruit big 'household name' charity organizations. We realized that smaller grass-roots organizations were doing fantastic things but struggling to raise enough funds to expand their reach. They worked closely with the local communities and consistently received feedback on the ground to improve their activities long term. But they didn't have a marketing department or access to good designers to attract more donors.

And the more we worked with small businesses and charities, the more we saw the real importance of connecting these little dots.

When a large amount of money goes to one big initiative and the activity gets implemented too quickly on a large scale, we usually don't see the possible consequences until it is too late and has actually become a big issue. So, the approach that everyone thought was right could, in fact, end up causing challenges in the communities that received the aid or support. It means that bigger initiatives have much greater responsibilities to stay closely in touch with what is really happening through the work they do and continuously re-align their methods with care and respect.

Of course, this does not lead to a conclusion that large organizations do not produce effective results. Big companies and large charity organizations with the agility, creativity and responsiveness that are more commonly seen in small organizations can create tremendous impact and positive change. In fact, many large companies and charities are trying to retain the innovative, creative and highly focused culture of a startup these days.

Bringing balance to our world by harnessing the *power of small and big* in the right combination is really the key to making the most impact.

The Power of Small

Another reason why smaller giving is superior to big giving is simply because it is more achievable. We often delay and procrastinate, especially when we aim to do something too big.

As I touched on earlier, many people (I was one of them!) think that they will do something great when they become successful. Some hope that they will travel and enjoy life when they retire. And some hope to spend more time with their family when they have more time in the future. Of course, it's easy to assume that we are not ready to do the things we want to do right now. But when we only look *forward* to doing the things we really want to do, we might never achieve them. And we are delaying the most desirable experiences to an indefinite future time.

Here's the fundamental question: *why not now?*

We can actually do what we want to do today if we are aiming to do smaller things. Can we not take a short time off work to visit a new place this month? Can we not pay more attention to the people around us and increase the quality of the time we can share today? If we break down our hopes and aspirations into small actions, we can easily achieve them and enjoy them regularly.

Giving is the same. If we think we can only give when we have a lot of money or time and when we believe that we can only give when we become successful, we will probably never give.

But if we give what we can today and help someone in a small way, we can already enjoy the positive benefits of giving; feeling more contented and grateful, right now.

If more and more people and businesses around the world started giving and sharing something small that they have today, it would invoke a far more powerful change than what one wealthy person, one big corporation or one government can do.

And if all these people and businesses increased their capacity to create a positive impact, we could see a massive change. We really can change our world together.

So in the following chapter, we are going to look at some very practical ways to increase your impact.

CHAPTER 4

GROWING YOUR TRIPLE IMPACT

> Success is not the key to happiness.
>
> Happiness is the key to success.
>
> If you love what you are doing, you will be successful.
>
> Albert Schweitzer

MAXIMIZING YOUR PERSONAL IMPACT

The Source of Your Triple Impact

Businesses with great impact are usually created and run by *people* with great impact.

And in your business, how *you* behave and make decisions personally impacts everyone and everything.

So in this chapter, we'll look into how you can grow and maximize your impact as a whole. Specifically, we are going to look into 3 key areas of your impact: your **personal impact**, your **social impact** and your **enterprise impact**.

These three types of impact are interconnected. And growing all three types of your impact allows you to experience the most rewarding journey in this meaning-driven world.

And your personal impact is where it all begins. It is the source of all the impacts you create in all areas of your existence. People with great personal impact live fulfilling and high-achieving lives while creating an environment for others to thrive and prosper.

Impactful leaders understand that consequences of their actions and behaviors are far more important than those of external situations and conditions.

When you grow your personal impact, everything else flourishes.

Happy, energetic, productive, creative, daring and caring business leaders create more than a successful business. They create a happier world.

With all of that in mind, let's talk about how you can maximize your personal impact by elevating your capacity to do good; how you can shift your own paradigm.

The Paradigm Shift

A *Paradigm Shift* happens when you shift your perceptions.

The widely known '*Maslow's Hierarchy of Needs*' explains how we are lifted to higher levels of needs as we experience the fulfillment of more basic needs.[31]

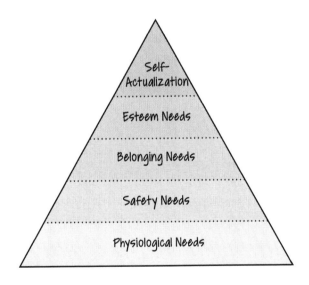

When we have nothing, our immediate need is to fulfill our physiological requirements. We need air to breathe, food to eat and water to drink.

We also need shelter and clothing for basic comfort. Once our physiological needs are relatively satisfied, we seek improved safety and security. After our physiological and safety needs are fulfilled, we seek a sense of belonging. When we are fulfilled with the bonds we form with others, we start finding our own identity and significance. And when all our personal needs are met, we strive to reach our greatest potential; to maximize the meaning of our own lives.

The fact that you are reading this book suggests that you are looking for ways to reach your full potential; to create positive impact on the world around you. It's a very natural progression to seek greater meaning in your life.

In a similar way, the highest aim of human civilization is **not** to create a society where everyone is worrying about how to get food and shelter to fulfill their own basic physiological needs. We belong to a civilization that can care for the wellbeing of all and use our collective knowledge, wisdom and skills to solve challenges we face together, to create a place where every one of us can reach our greatest potential.

It's nice to say that. But if we are to actually create such a world, we need to know how we can become the best we can be and help others reach their best too.

The Natural Cycle, Flow and Expansion of Life

There are natural cycles in our world just like the seasons and planetary cycles we looked at earlier.

In our lives too, there are cycles that we already live with. Here is one of those cycles.

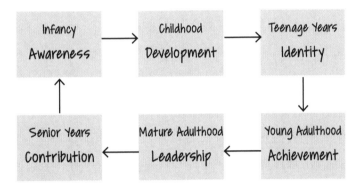

In life, all of us move through a cycle like this. We have a different focus at different ages. Young children are more focused on discovering the world and growing to gain new abilities. And as we age, our focus in life changes quite naturally.

Fully experiencing all of these developmental stages makes our lives more meaningful and fulfilling. And you can actually live this cycle many times over and experience the fullness of the world much more.

Some people don't move through this process very well. They get stuck somewhere. So they might not even experience one full cycle in their lifetime.

The good news is that we don't need to wait until we become older to move into the next phase. You can accomplish more at a younger age if you experience and master each element of this cycle. This way, you will have many more years of living life at what some refer to as a 'peak state'.

There are other cycles that are useful for you to understand to experience life at a peak state. Luckily, our ancestors and predecessors have left many clues for us to grasp many of these ideas in simple ways.

To make it easy for you, I have combined many of those concepts and philosophies into one simple diagram. It allows you to visualize the flow of your life and see how each component of your life affects others.

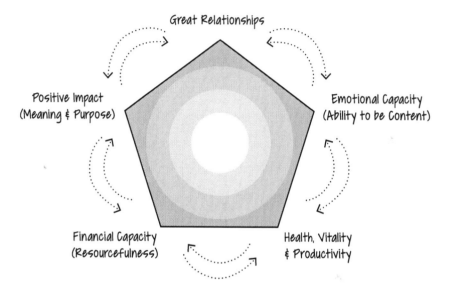

Let's call this diagram: 'The Flow of Life'.

In this model, our lives consist of five key components. And all five are interconnected. You cannot grow just one area of your life to reach your maximum potential. And if there is one area that is significantly compromised, the remaining areas of your life are affected too.

For example, having great relationships with others around you leads you to grow your emotional capacity more easily. And that leads to better health and increased productivity. If you are being productive and creating value for others, you are more likely to be better equipped with financial capacity too. And when you are sharing the abundance you have to benefit others, you increase your ability to build even greater relationships with others (and often with yourself).

This cycle continues to improve each and every component of your life and well-being gradually.

Now, let's take a look at another pattern.

Going Against the Flow

Let's say you are doing relatively well in life, and at one point, you start developing significant relationship issues with people close to you. I'm sure you can imagine what would happen after that. Your emotional capacity gets compromised first. And this can lead to health issues as you find it hard to relax, sleep or even eat properly. Experiencing severe emotional imbalance for a prolonged period can cause many physical issues even if you are generally a healthy person.

And if you are not healthy, how can you be productive, add value to others, and earn at your maximum capacity? And if you start asking for financial help continuously or are dependent and insecure, how would you be in the best possible space to make positive contributions and care for others?

On the other hand, if we suddenly gain a steep increase in one area without the balanced growth in all other areas, we could experience an adverse effect.

For example, people may suddenly acquire a lot of money winning the lottery even though they didn't establish financial capacity through their own effort. And if they don't figure out ways to sustainably use their wealth to benefit others as well as their own well-being, then this new sudden wealth could damage the relationships they have with others and eventually lead to other challenges.

People receiving a diagnosis of life-threatening disease can suddenly lose independence and productivity, and if they are not prepared for it, every other aspect of their life could be compromised. However, people who receive the same diagnosis might recover and even have a positive healing experience when they have great foundation in all other areas.

The Key Driver of Personal Impact

So, what can we do to create a great Flow of Life? The way to actually grow the stability of your overall wellbeing takes time and continuous effort. What it really takes is the *ability to improve*.

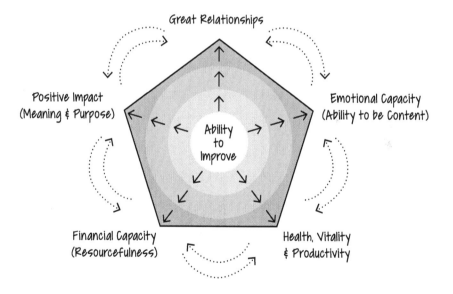

This simple cycle outlines how life is never about having overnight success. The ability we have to improve each area of our lives as we move in a circular motion through this life-long journey is the key to sustainably growing each aspect of our lives.

Unfortunately, there is no single magic pill you can take to change the way you feel about your life forever. Even winning the lottery does not fix all your problems.

It's you who has the power to grow your life every second, every day and in every way. And there is a simple model you can follow to maximize the outcome of your intentions.

The Formula for Creating Great Results

If it is about improving each area of our lives in each cycle, what can we do to obtain the ability necessary so that we can keep creating great outcomes?

Here are the steps to do that successfully and sustainably.

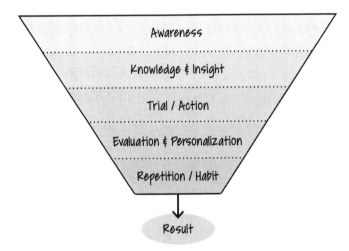

This is a funnel for creating the outcomes you desire. Let's call it: 'The Success Funnel'. A funnel normally filters and directs things in a downward movement through gravity. The quantity and the quality of substances that come out from the bottom of the funnel are determined by the structure of the funnel (and by what you pour into the funnel).

Funnel visualization is often used for evaluating the success of campaigns like marketing campaigns. You monitor how many 'hits' you get on your website, how many of them eventually convert to become your paying customers, and how many of them stay with you over a long period.

The concept of your Success Funnel is similar to that of many other funnel visualization models. The outcome of your experiences and actions are determined by the structure of the funnel you create and what you pour into this funnel. These results are continuously created whether you pay attention to them or not.

Success by Design

What you pour into the top of this funnel is mostly up to you. Sometimes, you might not be in control of what goes in. But what comes out of the bottom is determined by the funnel you design. You take in certain information from your surroundings, and that leads to specific thoughts, actions and outcomes.

Awareness

Sometimes, we are more conscious of our efforts to create the desired results. Other times, we think and act passively or reactively without realizing what's happening. Becoming aware of our surroundings, noticing an issue, spotting an opportunity and understanding our fundamental desires are excellent ways to grow our funnel. But becoming aware is not about becoming judgmental towards ourselves and others. Negative judgment leads to actions that do not contribute to the desired results. Objective consciousness leads to a greater capacity to create and improve things.

Knowledge and Insight

When we become aware of the things that matter to us, how much time and effort we allocate towards attaining the relevant information is critical. For example, do you spend more time reading newspapers, tuning in to social media and watching TV just to be in touch with all the general news and trends? Or do you spend more time tuning into specific information and exchanging ideas with the people who are experts in the field that's relevant to you? Building knowledge that matters to you helps you shape ideas and insights that impact lives; yours and those around you.

Trial / Action

Once we gain knowledge and insight, we can maximize the volume and quality of the flow by actually taking relevant action. Having a lot of knowledge but not putting it into action does not help us produce the results we want. And if you pay attention to too many irrelevant things and take action passively or reactively, you will not achieve the desired outcome.

Evaluation and Personalization

No single method or approach works for all. We are all different. So, one thing done by someone in a specific situation might not be suited to others. Everything you do needs to be evaluated and customized until you find your very own formula. And if you continue taking actions without taking a moment to evaluate them, you might end up creating habits that do not lead to your desired outcomes.

Repetition → Habit

And no matter how hard you act and learn, you will not

experience the long-term positive results and impact unless you can turn those well-aligned actions into a habit and part of your identity. This is often the most overlooked element of the success methodology. It's the part that requires discipline and conscious effort.

Result

Now you can be in charge of experiencing the expected results more consistently. But the most important thing here is how you actually recognize and appreciate the results you experience because that's what makes all your effort more meaningful.

And once you get results, you go back to the opening of another funnel. Many funnels can exist simultaneously too. This way, we continue to build our awareness, discover new information, take new actions, re-align our habits and appreciate greater outcome... all the while enjoying the whole experience.

Life is an ongoing journey.

Growing Your Personal Impact

What happens at each layer of the funnel is critical in maximizing the quality and the quantity of the outcomes you experience.

If you want to maximize your output without doing too much, you need to increase the quality and effectiveness of the funnel. If you are not experiencing what you want to have in life and business, you are probably making mistakes in at least one or more parts of your funnel. If you feel unhappy about what you are experiencing, your funnel is likely clogged with judgment or complacency.

It also means that you can consistently obtain greater results in everything you aspire to achieve just by establishing better funnels in all five areas of your life.

And let's highlight that one of the most overlooked elements of the Flow of Life: it's the fifth element, 'Positive Impact'.

Most people know that they need to have great relationships to fully enjoy their lives. They also know the importance of their mental, physical and financial health. But some people don't realize how their lives can become far more meaningful when they implement actions that create great positive impact. And they can do this easily by adding the focus of giving and caring.

If you continue to maximize the outcome in each of these five areas of your life by building great funnels, and keep improving them through each and every cycle of your journey, you will become unstoppable.

ENHANCING YOUR SOCIAL IMPACT

It's a common adage that you are the average of the five people you spend the most time with.

In the book '*Connected—The surprising power of our Social Networks*', two renowned social scientists, Nicholas A. Christakis and James H. Fowler explore the power of our connections through numerous social studies focusing on the power of social contagions.[32]

In one of their studies, Christakis and Fowler mapped out the relationship of 12,067 people with more than 50,000 ties (or connections between friends and relatives) among them. Analyzing the network, the authors noticed that obese people tend to be friends with other obese people while thin people tend to be friends with other thin people. Based on their reading of the data, the authors concluded that associating with overweight people, even indirectly, is likely going to make you overweight.

Time after time, after gathering and analyzing a wide variety of data from tens of thousands of people, the duo reached the same conclusion regarding the power of social connections that we form.

> "*Most of us are already aware of the direct effect we have on our friends and family; our actions can make them happy or sad, healthy or sick, even rich or poor. But we rarely consider that everything we think, feel, do, or say can spread far beyond the people we know. Conversely, our friends and family serve as*

conduits for us to be influenced by hundreds or even thousands of other people. In a kind of social chain reaction, we can be deeply affected by events we do not witness that happen to people we do not know. It is as if we can feel the pulse of the social world around us and respond to its persistent rhythms. As part of a social network, we transcend ourselves, for good or ill, and become a part of something much larger. We are connected."

We are, indeed, connected.

And we are connected more than ever before as we gain greater ability to interact and connect through the power of online media and affordable communication channels. There has never been a time like this.

You as an Influencer

What you think, do, and share can create greater consequences in the wider world. And who you choose to interact with, spend time with and work with significantly influences you. These people help you form who you are as much as you help them form who they are.

And while we all have different communication and leadership styles, consciously interacting with others makes us all better leaders and influencers. To enhance your positive social impact, you can start by understanding these three key things:

1. You cannot force others to change.
No matter how hard you try, you cannot force others to change. In fact, the harder you try to change others, the harder it becomes to change anyone.

The most effortless way for you to positively influence others is to change yourself first. If you see people behaving in ways you do not like, then instead of trying to change them, you can think of what's making them act in that way and find the means to make a positive difference in the situation. Instead of complaining, you can try to do more of the things you want others to do and stop doing things that you don't want others to do.

By accepting what people do and then transforming how **you** behave and act, you can more effectively transform what is happening around you.

2. What you do when no one is watching has a greater influence than what you do right in front of others.

Many people think that they can influence others by saying or doing things that are impressive or convincing. Well, that's partly true. But nothing can be more influential than what you do when no one is watching. This relates to the first point.

What you think and do when no one is watching is the *real* you (the outcome of your Success Funnel). When you begin transforming your influence internally first, the social impact you create becomes unshakable. You are clear about the decisions you make, and you are congruent with your own words.

Leaders who act consistently whether anyone is watching or not can lead a group with confidence and authenticity. And authentic leaders create a far more positive impact than leaders who speak powerfully and yet do not deliver.

3. No one likes to be judged. Everyone wants to be valued.

Even though it would be nice to be in a world where everyone takes criticism and feedback positively all the time, the reality is that no one really likes to be criticized. It is not that we do not want to change but criticism makes us more resistant to change. So, if we are to guide others toward a shared direction, a common goal, it's easier to lead via positive recognition, encouragement and appreciation.

As I said earlier, what's appreciated appreciates. At the same time, constructive and honest feedback works miracles in certain situations, especially when you have solid trusting relationships with the people around you (more on this on page 58). So, investing time and effort to build healthy relationships with others enables you to communicate more effectively and create greater long-term impact.

Keeping these things in mind enables you to improve your personal impact further and also allows you to help others enhance their personal impact, forming happier and more fulfilled social circles, workplaces and communities that create more positive impact across the board.

Your Social Footprint

Your social impact also involves what happens as a result of your existence; your social footprint. Take the things you choose to buy and the things you throw away, or the movies you decide to watch and the resources you consume each day.

You are creating a chain of social impacts just by living and doing what you do even when you are not thinking about it. And because of the way everything is produced, transported and sold these days, there is no way we could live an entirely isolated life where we do not benefit from or impact (positively and negatively) many other lives around the world.

The clothes you are wearing right now were produced somewhere by someone. The shirt you have on could have been produced by the mother of three healthy children happily working at home and earning extra income; she may be feeling proud to send her children to school because she didn't have the chance to attend school when she was young... Or, it could have been produced by a young mother who has to leave her young baby with her relatives to work in a cramped factory in a distant city because she has no choice, as her husband was seriously injured in an accident at the factory where he used to work...

Behind every decision you make is a myriad of very personal stories. And your choice to buy, sell or use an item means you're inevitably choosing to be part of the web of countless stories across the globe.

You are voting to shape the world in a certain way with every action and choice you make.

Voting for Businesses That Care

Often, people think that being socially conscious means being part of an activist group, becoming vegan or joining a protest movement. But these actions might not always resonate with you. In this complex, interconnected world, trying to be right by rejecting everything we do not agree with or arguing to prove what's right and wrong is often challenging.

A far easier and effective way to create the change we want to see is to support and acknowledge people, organizations and businesses that demonstrate the behaviors that we admire.

When we choose products and services based purely on lower prices, we are encouraging suppliers of those products and services to focus on the maximization of profits.

The companies that are cutting corners today cannot be solely blamed when the market supports them for providing cheaper products, even at the expense of so many things.

Many years ago, we had access to very limited information. So, when corporate scandals were exposed, we could simply say that we didn't know what was really happening behind the scenes. We could just blame the companies and their decision-makers. But today, we have greater ability to find the facts when we spend a little extra time. And today we have a choice.

Do we read the labels of the products we regularly buy? Do we search for other alternatives that are in line with our own beliefs? Do we visit the websites of companies and find out what they care about before deciding that their products are too expensive?

While businesses are expected to improve their communications in this connected world, we as consumers have the opportunity to take a moment and explore the stories behind the businesses. If we made a small investment of time to support the companies that cared more, if we took the opportunity to buy as if it's a vote we cast with our money, we would create a world where caring and honesty becomes part of the important business values.

Your social impact is enhanced every day—by every thought you hold, every choice you make and every action you take.

DRIVING YOUR ENTERPRISE IMPACT

If we want to create a successful life by accomplishing great things and by feeling fulfilled in the process, we should be able to build successful businesses by doing the same things: creating great impact AND experiencing a sense of fulfillment on an ongoing basis.

Businesses are created and run by people, so it is understandable that the journey of a business is just like the journey of a human life. Businesses at the fundamental level are the same as human beings.

It means that concepts like 'Maslow's Hierarchy of Needs' apply to businesses as well.

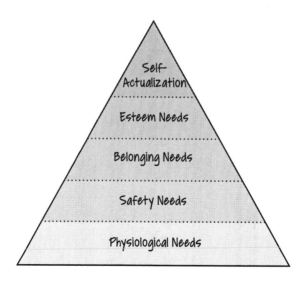

When businesses begin a journey, they too need to fulfill their physiological requirements first. They need funds; they need products and services to sell. And they need to create sales transactions. They also need manpower, systems and processes to keep delivering the value. Once their physiological needs are met, they require stable cash flow and a healthy business environment. After that, they seek to create a greater sense of connection with their customers and employees. When these needs are fulfilled, businesses would also seek their own identity and significance.

So ultimately, businesses can aspire to reach their greatest potential—to maximize the meaning of their own existence—just like we do as individuals.

Starting a Business With a Reason

At a very fundamental level, a business can start its journey with the simple aim of fulfilling the basic needs of the owner and his or her family. It first has to tackle the issue of its own sustainability.

Many businesses fail at this stage. But fundamentally, it is not too hard to simply survive as a business if what you're selling is valued at more than what it costs the business to provide those products or services. Many small family businesses can continue for years simply at this level.

Beyond this point, some businesses go on to start generating more than enough cash flow and accumulate assets to create greater security.

But once the business becomes sustainable, it requires a sense of purpose to grow further. That's partly because people who are working for these businesses will eventually start seeking more than just stable jobs and paychecks. So, these businesses have to be willing to reach the next level in Maslow's model to retain a quality workforce.

Starting a business to meet merely your physiological needs is not a great choice to make these days. If you just want more income and security, working as an employee can often be a far better and much easier option.

So, instead of just trying to meet basic financial needs, today's businesses should exist to offer greater value—special reasons for their existence. They still need to work on making money, of course. But making money allows them to make more of the invaluable things they can offer, not just for surviving and providing financial security for the owners.

The 'Flow of Business'

Just like individuals, businesses go through cycles of growth. And it turns out that we can broadly define five main areas in the business development cycle too.

This slightly adjusted chart (similar to the one for the Flow of Life cycle on page 113) describes the flow and the process of business growth.

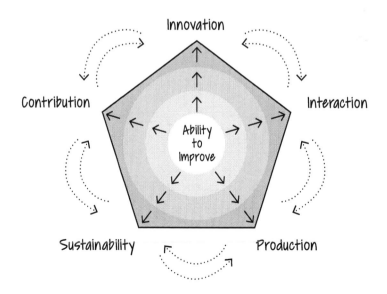

Every business starts with a concept: an idea (**Innovation**). And a good idea that's expressed well to engage (**Interaction**) will gain momentum. And by delivering on the promise and exceeding expectations (**Production**), happy customers are created and more business flows in. And when the business process becomes consistent and efficient (**Sustainability**), positive cash flow is created and profitability stabilizes. And finally, the meaning of the business is maximized when it creates a positive impact; when it goes beyond just making money (**Contribution**). This fifth element of 'Contribution' (which is often seen as low priority) is what differentiates businesses today.

Adding effective giving and caring in your business is one of the most impactful things you can do. It creates a great culture that lasts. And it makes a difference in all areas of your business development journey.

When your business is focused on growing all of these five areas together as a whole, it becomes a real Giving Business.

Growing a Business, Sustainably

In order to maximize the ability for your business to keep growing throughout this cycle, you need to design and improve your Success Funnels in all of these five areas of your business.

The structure of the Success Funnel used here is the same as what you saw earlier to improve your personal impact.

To keep creating great results in business, you need to be aware of what's happening in the specific areas of your business, and you need to gain relevant knowledge and insight to respond to situations and opportunities. You then need to take appropriate actions to see how they make a difference.

Once you find a great model/strategy that works for you, you can create systems and processes to make them part of your regular, repeatable activities.

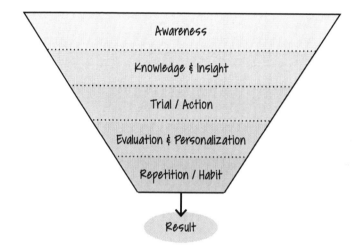

When you repeat this process effectively and design great Success Funnels around your business, you create high-impact business activities. And at the completion of each cycle to improve the five areas of your business, you start a new cycle of development.

It's an ongoing journey.

Maximizing the Meaning of Your Business

If you're growing your business steadily and enjoying what you do, we can say you're already doing well. But for your business to maximize the *meaning* of what you do, you need to be more than just doing well.

So, what makes the difference between businesses that are simply doing well and those that are creating exceptional value and are loved by their customers?

There are three key components for achieving this and creating a business that matters.

↗ *The type of value you create*

↗ *The way you deliver that value*

↗ *The way you connect with the stakeholders*

Now, let's look at how this 'triple focus' helps you drive your enterprise impact—the true meaning of your business.

Crafting Value

The first component we can work on is the type of value you create.

To do this in the best possible way, you can think of your business as an agent to help people and organizations experience greatness in their own journeys.

We've already seen that our lives can be continuously improved by growing the five key areas: by creating **Great Relationships**, by establishing **Emotional Capacity**, by improving **Health, Vitality and Productivity**, by attaining **Financial Capacity** and by increasing the **Positive Impact** we create.

If your products and services help people develop one or more of these areas effectively, you are adding meaningful value. What you are offering has greater meaning than just fulfilling any need.

And if your business serves other businesses and organizations (so-called B2B business), you can focus on helping your clients improve one or more of the five areas of their business development: **Innovation, Interaction, Production, Sustainability** and **Contribution**.

When you help your customers and clients accomplish things that matter to them the most, what you offer will naturally have more positive impact, both directly and indirectly.

Delivering Value

The second component for creating a meaningful business is the way you deliver the value you provide. The methodology for this is quite simple: you use your Success Funnel again.

If you are designing a great Success Funnel to deliver your value so that your customers can experience real results, they will come back for more, and they will stay with you.

Creating a business with greater meaning requires effective delivery of value that benefits people. If you really want to make a difference, you want to help your customers experience real results. And to effectively do so, you need a great Success Funnel to raise awareness, offer useful information, give relevant action points, let people personalize their approach and help them create beneficial habits.

You can also work with other businesses to provide complete, long-term solutions for your customers. This way, you don't need to offer all the elements of the Success Funnel. You can simply form symbiotic partnerships with other businesses to help your customers succeed.

For example, if you provide raw ingredients for healthy meals (*e.g.* if you are a farmer wanting to help people become healthy), you can provide your products to a health food wholesaler and they can supply your products to retail stores, online delivery businesses and restaurants that focus on healthy eating. You can write articles about how to create a healthy eating habit and distribute the information via various media outlets. You might even partner with local schools and businesses to educate people about the importance of healthy eating.

These partnerships enable you to reach and serve a greater number of people who want to become and stay healthy.

Knowing precisely where your business fits into the whole solution makes what you do more focused on your niche and helps you become clear about with whom you want to partner.

Connecting Through Meaning

Aside from delivering direct value to their customers, businesses also provide opportunities to a larger network of people. They offer jobs to people so that they can earn income from their work to sustain their lives. Many businesses also offer investment opportunities so that people with resources can leverage on the capital they have. They also offer a variety of opportunities to their partners and suppliers.

Giving Businesses go much further.

They use the third component of creating a meaningful business—looking deeper at the way they connect with all of their stakeholders.

How you maximize meaning for all of your stakeholders is part of driving your enterprise impact to the fullest extent. And it mostly depends on how you are communicating your values with them.

For example, if you run an online shopping business, you might say your value and mission is *"to provide you with more convenience"* or you can identify it as *"to let you enjoy more quality time with your family"* or *"to give you the complete worry free solution so that you can focus on the things that matter."* You can see how different ways of communicating similar ideas can create very different feelings in the minds of people.

Maybe you can re-think and re-imagine **why** you are in business and how you want to share that with your stakeholders.

Every day, just by doing what you do, you are touching lives of people in deeper ways than you can imagine.

How you design your business and your enterprise impact makes a tremendous difference, for good.

WHEN ALL THREE IMPACTS MEET

When your personal, social and enterprise impacts come together, you embrace all aspects of your life and business as an integrated whole.

Increased personal impact naturally leads to increased social impact. And enterprises (businesses and other types of organizations) that are started and run by people with high personal and social impact create more significant impact commercially as well.

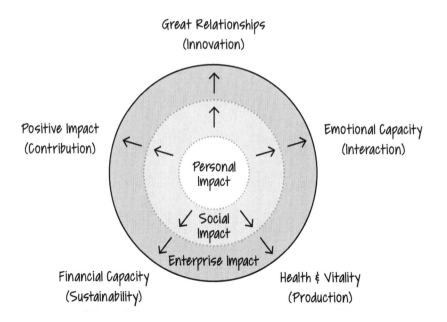

Your goal is to continuously grow all five aspects of your life and business that are needed to maximize the impact of your whole existence.

When you embody and grow your Triple Impact holistically, you no longer have clear divisions between you, your connections and your business. You value and nurture each and every element of your life. You are always on the lookout for opportunities to improve yourself, your environment, your connections and your work. You become an authentic leader who is always willing to serve a cause, who leads by example.

In fact, this is the only path to your true ongoing success—to maximize the impact of your life's work while experiencing the maximum sense of enjoyment, gratitude and fulfillment in doing what you do.

There is no better place to be than right here, at the center of our maximum Triple Impact.

THE IMPACT TEST

To get a better idea of how you can make the best improvements in maximizing your Triple Impact, you can try testing your current status and then find out your key areas for maximum improvement.

www.GivingBusiness.global/ImpactTest

Please use the special code **GBCTOKEN** to take the test so that you will receive the full report of your test results afterward for free.

I encourage you to read through this chapter again later as you keep moving through different stages of development, to really understand, design, refine and maximize the impact you create long term.

You are also welcome to share this test token with others you know. And I recommend that you share this book with them too so that they also experience the benefits of understanding the whole concept of Giving Business.

CHAPTER 5

MEASURING IMPACTS
THAT MATTER

The measure of who we are is
what we do with what we have.

Vince Lombardi

WHEN YOU MEASURE WRONG IMPACT

In our lives and in our businesses, we measure many things. Even if you are not a person who is passionate about spreadsheets, statistics, charts and graphs, you measure many things every day.

Why Measure?

People measure the time it takes to drive to work on a particular route, the amount of money they spend for a meal or the number of hours they sleep on a specific night. And often, much of that measurement is done unconsciously; we don't even know we're doing it.

The reason we measure things is to have a precise and clear perspective of something. We want to know what's bigger, what's faster, what's better or what's more efficient so that we can make sense of our world and our performance in it.

Unless we have a concept of time, we never know whether we are spending our time smartly. Unless we can compare with a clear measurement, we never know what to choose, what to expect or when to deliver.

Measurement is then a tool to help create a better sense of direction, a clearer communication with others, and a better sense of appreciation about our world and our lives. When we are using the power of measurement effectively, we can relate to what is happening in an empowering way and produce greater results, and have a greater sense of accomplishment.

There's a common management dictum: '*What you can measure, you can manage.*' But there is a problem; we can easily end up measuring the wrong things and, therefore, manage the wrong things too.

Being Confused by What to Measure

Sometimes, we measure many things that are irrelevant in relation to what we really want to achieve. There's an overwhelming amount of information available all the time. So, finding **what** we can measure is no challenge at all. But choosing what we actually measure in order to achieve desired outcomes is an enormous challenge because we have so many choices.

Consider this simple example: let's say your goal is to become healthy. There are so many things you can measure. You can choose to measure your weight, your blood pressure, your energy level or your physical strength. There are a thousand things you could measure that could possibly indicate your health status.

But one of these figures alone might not give you a clear perspective on the real state of your health because all these conditions are interconnected. And measuring certain things and then **reacting** to the findings might even work against you.

What Happens When We Measure Wrong Things

Because there are so many things you can measure, it is so easy to end up measuring the things that will not lead to your sense of real, meaningful achievement and satisfaction.

For example, many people count the number of friends they have on their social media accounts these days. But by being glued to the screen, they may have forgotten to measure the quality of relationships they have with people right around them.

And when we look at the measurement of money, most people think that measuring the amount of money they have in their bank accounts and managing their finances to accumulate enough money for their retirement is important (and it is). However, they might not measure the quality of experiences they are having each day to create the happy (and healthy) retirement they actually want.

Often, different people measure very different things with the same objective. For example, when people are bored by what they are doing at work, some of them measure the hours and minutes left in the work day (so that they can see that they are getting close to the end of the day) while some others measure interesting ideas they can come up with to improve the situation.

It shows how you are more likely or less likely to achieve what you want depending on what you are measuring. And to measure and act on the right things in your business, you need to first clarify what specific outcomes you are aiming to create.

Feeling Disconnected

Several of my business friends have expressed to me that they have felt a little disconnected from what they are doing in their businesses. When I asked them why, some of them said, "*Well, my business is a **normal** business. We are just selling what people need. There is nothing amazing or inspiring about what we do.*"

It appears to be that these people started to wonder at one point why they were in business at all. Having to do so much hard work, dealing with challenging issues and competing with many other businesses, they felt tired and disconnected because they've forgotten why they went into business in the first place. After all, they could be working for another business as an employee if they only wanted to earn enough (or more) money.

I've also met many business owners who are consistently enthusiastic about their businesses even though the type of business as they are operating could also be seen as conventional. They are fond of the process of developing their businesses strategically, facing challenges boldly and overcoming difficulties against all odds. Many of them are very much into the numbers their businesses are generating, and they closely monitor their progress, marketing trends, and competitors' moves.

I wondered what made the difference between these two groups of people. And I realized that it was simply the way they saw what they were doing—their own perception of the work they do.

Measuring the Things That Matter to You

The only way to really enjoy the game is to find meaning that matters to you, to find that 'thing' that makes it really your game. And that depends (like so many other things) on how we look at things—the lens through which we see the world.

Consider this 'what if': *what if we could see the stories of real people behind all those numbers and statistics?*

In your own game of business, you are the one to set your own goals, targets, and objectives. So these things are within your control. If you are in the wellness business, then you might want to set a goal to create as many happy people who are contented with their bodies and well-being as possible. If you are into book publishing, you could aim to spread positive stories and useful ideas to as many people as you can.

And if you don't feel good about the environmental distractions your industry is creating, you can target the number of trees you plant and protect, or number of stories you spread with an important message.

Then perhaps you could design better systems and processes to advance your mission—your own meaning—by understanding (and empathizing with) those stories right there in the depth and breadth of the data laid out before you.

When you find your own meaning in everything you do, it is possible to perceive that the challenges you encounter are simply obstacles popping up in the game. They are here to increase the meaning and enjoyment of the game you are playing.

After all, a game with no obstacles wouldn't be fun, would it?

PAINTING A PICTURE OF NEW POSSIBILITIES

Why the World is Becoming Faster

In recent years, the way systems interact with us has changed dramatically. What our smartphones can do today is astonishing compared to what we used to have even just a decade ago. And that is because of the data we collect, interpret and then apply to improve the systems we have.

People who study the movement of big data tell us that 2.5 quintillion bytes (that's 2,500,000,000,000,000,000 bytes) of data are created every day. This is as of 2015. By the time you read this book, that number will have already changed significantly.

Our ability to collect and store data is accelerating at lightning speed. Astonishingly, 90 percent of data we have in our world has been collected just within the last two years.[33]

We use the data to continuously improve our lives. It makes our lives more convenient, efficient and certainly much more fast-paced.

Data saves us money (now we can easily find the best deal available for a particular product, or find any information for free online), creates more money, connects us to our greater community, gives us a sense of clarity and so on.

When I travel today, I'm continuously astonished by what I see. People everywhere are becoming increasingly connected, often tuning in to the same sets of data no matter where they are. You find people using Facebook to interact with each other in the most remote communities in developing countries. And when you hop on a train anywhere in the world, you see people staring at their smartphone screens playing games, watching movies or tuning in to news and updates.

How to Use the Power of Data

Regardless of the vastness and the complexity of the data, the things we see and experience are presented in simpler ways, often with easy-to-assimilate infographics. This is just as well because we have less time and less patience these days as we get used to the faster flow of data that new technologies bring us.

Of course, we don't want to see the raw data and try to make sense of it ourselves. That's for the smart people in tech industries to figure out, isn't it?

But that brings with it an interesting challenge. Because of the sheer volume and complexity of the data, the people who generate it can also manipulate human behavior by misrepresenting the data.

Here's the reality: you can capture a lot of data points and easily throw away all the ones you don't want, and only keep those that support your position.

Managers and directors who receive incentives for boosting profits of the business might use the data to forecast and create short-term gains even if they see possible future consequences of the data. They don't have negative intentions; it's just the way they learned to play the game.

On the other hand, we can use accurately collated and beautifully presented data to solve challenging problems, make our lives significantly better, more comfortable, more secure and more fulfilling.

If we are the providers of the data, and we choose the right data to present to the right people at the right time for the right reason, we can positively influence people around the world from anywhere in the world. When you tell a compelling story with select data and paint a compelling picture, it can become a powerful agent of positive change.

Living in harmony with our technology and using it to do great things is the only way forward. All we need to do is commit to doing one thing...

Using our capabilities and resources to benefit all.

And while it is simple to say that, it may sound unrealistic. It might sound like you have to give up your possessions and move to a monastery.

Actually you don't. None of us do. We don't need to give up everything nor do we need to try to become saints.

In our families, we share what we have to benefit everyone in the family. So again it's just a matter of extending that boundary, or "drawing the circle bigger," as Mother Teresa put it.

You can explore two ideas that will help make sense of this.

➚ *There is a limit to the happiness money can provide.*

➚ *'Handed-down' or inherited financial prosperity does not create the same benefits as the wealth created by our own efforts.*

Leaving Money Vs. Leaving a Legacy

Many (if not most) people feel that they want to leave financial security for their children. All parents want their children to have happy lives.

And having plenty of money makes life easier.

But when it comes to happiness, study after study finds that people who have earned their wealth are happier than those who have inherited it.

A poll conducted by a financial management company in the US targeted more than 1,500 Americans with more than $500,000 in investible assets. It found that 76 percent of people who earned their wealth felt less stress and worry around financial matters, compared to 50 percent of those who had inherited their wealth. This same study also found that a full 50 percent of men and women who had inherited their wealth felt that it caused more problems than it solved.[34]

Subsequently, a Gallup survey of 450,000 Americans in 2008 and 2009 found that the ideal income for happiness, measured as 'day-to-day contentment', reached a plateau at $75,000. Until this level of income was achieved, there was a direct correlation between incremental increases in income and increases in happiness. After this point, people could acquire more 'stuff', but their happiness would reach a plateau.[35]

So, how about leaving a legacy of contribution as a part of the gift you leave for the people you care about?

Focusing on Overwhelming Issues

It's important for us to realize that there is enough to go around, that the world is actually capable of providing enough for everyone. All we have to do is contribute great value to others, be happy about what we have and be happy to share it.

It's sometimes not easy to see that. Sometimes we focus more on what we see as a lack of resources and uncertainty about our future.

And with that focus, the problems in our world can often seem too big and too complicated. Therefore, people only end up trying to get more and save more to ensure that they will not face scarcity themselves.

It comes back to that 'power of data' we spoke about earlier: how we focus on things depends on how things are presented to us. For example, some information presented today goes like this:

↗ *16,000 children die every day from preventable or treatable causes.*

↗ *Nearly half of all deaths in children under age 5 are attributable to malnutrition.*

↗ *More than 700,000 people do not have access to clean water.*

↗ *2.4 billion people lack access to adequate sanitation.*

↗ *Every 10 minutes, somewhere in the world, an adolescent girl dies as a result of violence.*

(Statistics from UNICEF)[36]

Those seem like massive issues, don't they?

And you probably don't think that you can help solve these issues. That's often the challenge of focusing on issues that are presented this way.

Equally, it's unlikely that you believe your own actions have anything to do with causing these realities. And the way the numbers are presented doesn't make us change our actions or our habits.

But what if we took a slightly different focus when looking at these big numbers?

The Power We Already Have

Now, let me give you another perspective.

Here are some statistics laid out in a totally different way. The chart below shows what was estimated as *additional* costs to achieve universal access to basic social services in all developing countries compared to sizes of various industries.

Global Priority	Additional Funds Required (yearly)*	Industry	Global Industry Size (yearly)**
Providing access to basic education	$22 billion	Media (Newspaper)	$168 billion
Providing adequate water and sanitation	$23 billion	Pharmaceutical	$1 trillion
Providing basic nutrition	$30 billion	Fast Food	$568 billion
Providing proper birth assistance	$12 billion	Cosmetics (Manufacturing)	$264 billion

*Global Priority Statistics (1998-2014) from
WHO[37], UNESCO[38] and GLOBAL ISSUES[39]
**Industry Statistics (2015) from IBIS World[40]

These Global Priority figures were estimated at various points of time. The actual cost of providing required support to people in developing countries would also vary depending on how the work is executed as well. Even so, the figures laid out in this way still show you a broad contrast of the cost of these basic requirements against the scale of our commercial activities.

Now, please pause for a moment and look at the numbers on the right side of this comparison again. Then you'll also see that the industries listed here are only a small part of our business world today. There are so many types of businesses in our world. Our lives are touched and influenced by many different business activities every day.

And this leads to a realization:

Businesses in our world have the power to solve our challenges.

Businesses are taking advantage of the technology and connectivity of today's world to achieve truly astonishing wealth. They can now easily import materials they don't have in their own countries at a very low cost, they can manufacture the products in a faraway place benefiting from lower labor costs, and they can export and distribute the products efficiently to many parts of the world.

What's actually missing is the right kind of connections and mechanisms for using this amazing financial power that we already have.

This is no longer just about how to implement good CSR (Corporate Social Responsibility) practices in large corporations. It is crucial that all businesses work together to solve the world's pressing issues. This is the shared responsibility they must take in this connected world.

And if you are running or working for a business, you are also representing one of these businesses that can lead the change. And it is our fundamental human responsibility to care for our race.

As customers and clients of businesses, we also have the power to choose to support businesses that are making an effort to contribute towards the sustainability of our world.

We can create significant improvements for the wellbeing of all citizens of our world when we learn to direct the power of data (knowledge), technology (tools), business activities (transactions) and purchasing choices (investment) that we already have.

There is surely no greater mission than this.

Painting a Picture of New Possibilities

Imagine a world where all children are given equal opportunities to experience a childhood where they can play, learn and connect with one another without fear. A world where they can enjoy healthy nourishing meals with their families, where they have access to clean drinking water, proper sanitation and good medical care. A world where they can use their own talents to the fullest and find occupations and professions they love so that they can contribute to the greater good of the humanity and the world's natural beauty that we share.

Imagine a world where everyone is trying to make positive contributions to their communities, to help people who have less so that we all have more.

This is the world we can create just by shifting our focus to the direction we want to head towards. And our businesses have the power to create that world already.

Better yet, it's actually very simple to do. In the next section, we are going to break down these big global priorities into small things that we can make happen.

THE POWER OF SMALL: WHAT ONE DOLLAR CAN DO

Our Relationship With Money

Some people have difficulty with money. Money is sometimes described as 'the root of all evil'.

Yet it seems that everyone is trying to get more of it.

Whether we like it or not, our world is very much driven by money. And the truth is, using it in the right way can be a tremendous source of good.

For the moment, let's just look at money in the context of impact. And soon we'll look at some amazing things that just one dollar can do.

Measuring Your Business Impact

There are so many ways to measure your business outcomes. You can, of course, measure the amount of money you make and the amount of money you spend.

You can also count the number of products or services you sell. You can count the number of customers, the frequency of transactions, the average number of transactions per customer or average customer spending per transaction. You can measure the quality of your customer's experience through polls and surveys as well. There is no shortage of ways to evaluate your business' impact.

Money is definitely one of the most important resources we all measure, monitor and create in business. You need more of it to grow your business, and you measure the size and quality of the value you are creating in monetary amounts. You can test whether people are willing to pay for the price you are asking. Money is the universal currency for exchanging value in the marketplace. It's the only thing that you officially and legally need to measure and report to the government to stay in business as well.

But what you might not be familiar with yet is the hidden power of money in our world. Knowing this gives you a new way to understand the power your business has no matter how big or small it is.

What You Might Do With One Dollar

If you had a spare dollar right now, what would you do with it?

You might go and buy a copy of today's newspaper. You might drop it in your piggy bank as spare change. You might purchase a music track on iTunes. Or you might give it to a person standing across the road collecting donations.

In your business, if you had one extra dollar, what would you do? Or if you had one extra dollar in your net profit per product sale, what would you do with it? You might give a discount to your customer. You might improve the packaging of the product. Or you might improve your marketing efforts to sell more product. There are so many other ways you can invest that one extra dollar.

One of those ways you might consider is prosocial spending (see page 79) to become happier and more fulfilled. So, what can one dollar really do?

And if you look at what we might call 'traditional' giving, you might think the answer is 'not very much.' We don't tend to think in small numbers when it comes to giving.

Breaking Down to the Smallest Impact

Through the work we do at Buy1GIVE1, we've had the opportunity to meet with representatives from many charity organizations. We have faced many situations where we were asked to raise a large sum of money. It's not uncommon to be asked something like this: *"our organization needs to raise $1.5 million dollars to build a new school. Can you help?"*

Our answer to these kinds of questions is almost always *"No."* Because it's not what we are focused on doing here. We do not promise to raise large amounts of funds for future projects.

Fortunately, there are other ways of raising funds and grants from large corporations and governments that can help these organizations raise enough money for their significant projects. Big giving trends like the 'Ice Bucket Challenge' or annual campaigns/events like 'Movember' (also known as No-shave November) have raised millions for their specific featured causes. And there are crowd-funding sites that help people and organizations raise a significant amount of funds for their startup initiatives.

Buy1GIVE1 has a different focus. As we said, it's about *the Power of Small*: about making small things happen regularly to create significant long-term results.

So, what we look for are activities that are happening regularly. We look for grassroots charity organizations with effective projects, transparency and good financial management practices. The projects we list have to have a track record of improving a specific issue in their own community for at least three years.[41] Once we find these projects, we work with the organizations to break down their projects into small micro-giving units.

For example, let's say we are looking at working with an NGO in Ethiopia which has been building wells in rural communities for many years. We first identify the average cost of building one well, including the maintenance cost (unless other funding covers the maintenance). We then identify the average lifespan of their wells and how many people live in an average-sized community. Once we find out these numbers, we can start dissecting and breaking down the project. In this case, we can find out the cost of providing access to a well for one person, for one year, one month, one week and one day.

In many cases, the cost of the smallest unit can be as low as just a few cents. And this leads back to that earlier question: *so, what can one dollar do?*

What One Dollar Can Do

Here are some of the impacts you can create by giving just one dollar:

(amount in USD as at April 2016)[42]

↗ *100 days of access to life-saving water for one person (Ethiopia)*

↗ *a nourishing meal for four child refugees to boost their nutrition (Thailand)*

↗ *access to a playground for a schoolchild for four months (Cambodia)*

↗ *support for a slum child to attend school for three days (India)*

↗ *medication to care for one sick person for two days (Ukraine)*

↗   *a pair of glasses (Indonesia)*

↗   *one day of access to a computer room for one indigenous woman (Australia)*

There are many other things you can do with just one dollar or less (*see more: www.b1g1.com/projects*).

Of course, the cost and types of activities vary from one country to another. These examples merely illustrate how little it takes for you to make a difference in many tangible ways. It shows how **you** can start tackling the issues we have in our world by making small differences right now.

Imagine what can be achieved if everyone put aside just a small amount to give regularly.

Sharing the Gratitude

When we imagined a world full of giving, where everything we do makes a difference in a 'buy one give one' way, we thought it was the best idea ever. We thought this could become the way for businesses to 'pollinate the world' just like the bees do.

When we add special giving to our activities, having a nice meal with friends becomes an even more meaningful and enjoyable experience. Serving one more customer becomes more meaningful and rewarding for you and your team too.

When we feel grateful, we can truly enjoy the things we love without feeling guilty. We might also feel less attached to having more and more things. And we might feel happy to spend a little more on the things that matter to us. When you imagine the joy you can bring to those who are less fortunate than you by giving and sharing a little more, you appreciate everything in your life even more too.

Businesses that we work with are linking many meaningful giving activities to their everyday business activities. They ensure that every time they do business (*e.g.* every time they sell one of their products or services), something great happens as a direct result.

When businesses add a special meaning to their small everyday activities like this, measuring the impacts long-term becomes truly rewarding. Imagine the smiles you can create every day just by doing what you normally do.

Giving, or prosocial spending, is a great way for you to feel a sense of purpose, and a sense of fulfillment in life and business. It's a way to celebrate your small wins along the way and to express your gratitude to the people who make what you do possible as well.

When you are running a Giving Business, the more you achieve, the bigger impact you create for many others. You now have a greater reason to succeed. And you can even help create a happier world in many special ways.

THE BUSINESS OF BEING YOU

Now you see the importance of having your clear WHY, the importance of having a giving focus, the importance of your balanced Triple Impact and the importance of measuring and acting on the right information.

All these things contribute to the journey of a Giving Business.

But seeing and feeling the true reason and meaning to be in business might not come naturally to everyone. Some people may find it hard to see that they have something very special to offer. They might feel that other successful business owners and famous CEOs reached great heights because they had truly unique qualities or that they were exceptionally lucky or gifted.

Your Unique DNA

The reality is that no one is so gifted by nature. Even our DNA is 99.9 percent the same as everyone else's. Biologically and physically, we were born with very similar features and capabilities.

But that small difference is still remarkable. Within that tiny 0.1 percent difference that you and I have in our DNA, there are more than three million variations between your genome and anyone else's. And because of the mutations that randomly and consistently occur at every reproductive cycle (each person's genome contains about 100 mutations on average), we all carry a unique sequence of DNA that's different from everyone else's—even from our siblings'.

And what make us truly unique on top of our physical differences are our different upbringings and experiences. We have lived in various places, received different education, made numerous mistakes, learned different lessons. We have been influenced by different mixes of people, cultures, languages, beliefs and traditions. We have established different styles, skills, characteristics and capabilities through those unique experiences we had.

As a unique individual, you're not supposed to live your life the same way others might choose to live. And your choice to start a particular business at a specific time brings a new meaning to the world.

Your Business in the Global Eco-System

Scientists and biologists tell us that every element and living thing that exists in our world plays a role in the balance of our eco-system. They also say that all the elements in our bodies, including our cells, tissues and organs play vital roles for maintaining our biological balance.

And in much the same way, people and businesses that exist in our world are interconnected, playing different roles in the maintenance of the unique balance of our cultures, our histories and our future direction. No single entity is to be ignored and disregarded.

You, as a unique individual, play a very special and important role in the eco-system of our society and our world too. You are the only person in the whole world who can feel, think, act and influence like you do.

And your business is an expression of you and the many others whose lives it touches. So, when you can be true to your own meaning throughout your business endeavors, you inspire and empower others to find their own meaning and stay true to it as well.

The most important understanding you can have is the value of your own *meaning*. With appreciation for your own uniqueness and the role you play, you can continue to do your best in maximizing your positive impact.

This is the essence of your Giving Business: a business that truly matters. By harnessing the power of giving, it can thrive in this new meaning-driven world.

I hope that by reading this book, you have gained additional clarity, connected more with your true purpose and learned new ways to enjoy your journey as a person and as a business leader.

Imagine playing a part in creating a world that you truly want to belong to. And now, you really can.

REFLECTIONS

ONE FINAL STORY...

When I speak at events, one of the questions I often receive is this: *"What's the biggest challenge you've faced in your entrepreneurial journey?"*

I think this is because these questions often serve people in the audience better than lectures or presentations do. We learn more effectively from other people's stories. And hearing about the challenges others had and how they overcame them can help each of us make sense of our own challenges and show us the way to our greatest potential.

When I look back, I find no shortage of stories of failures and challenges. And today, I want to share one story (which I don't share often) as the final piece of this book to highlight the power of giving, in a very personal way.

Sometimes, Life Brings Challenges

As I mentioned briefly in this book, I used to have a food business in Australia before I co-founded B1G1 and moved to Singapore to run the initiative.

And the reason we (my ex-partner, David, and I) started the food business and worked so hard for it was because we both wanted to do something meaningful. We wanted to help children around the world who had been born in trying circumstances. We were planning to give away all the profits to help feed and educate underprivileged children.

But during the early stages of running the business, we faced many challenges. Some of the challenges were overwhelming for me as I was also learning to be a mother for the first time. And one of the underlying issues we had was a very common one: a severe lack of funding.

Because we started the business with little capital and we were inexperienced in business management, even our greatest ideas didn't flourish easily. In addition, the idea we had at first, an online shop for home delivery of organic and gluten-free meals, was probably a little too early for the market at that time. People were not ordering meals online yet. And home delivery was only common for pizza businesses. And even pizza businesses operated predominantly by taking phone orders.

But I also had a bigger problem.

We were two and a half years into the business journey when we leased a large industrial unit and started building our new kitchen. And just then, I discovered that I was pregnant again.

At that time, I was a resident of Australia but without access to public medical care. And we didn't even have money to go to the hospital —I saved every penny from our personal spending to pay for business expenses. And we were too busy to be thinking about another baby coming into our lives.

I kept working 16 hours a day, seven days a week. I got up at 2 a.m. on weekends to sell our products at Farmers' Markets because our online sales could not possibly cover the entire cost of running the business.

No matter how tired I was, I kept on working like this. It was because I could always think of those people and children who had very little and yet still offered to share their meals with me when I was traveling as a young and vulnerable foreigner. I felt that my own challenges were nothing compared to what they were dealing with.

A Great Idea…?!

My optimism was stretched to the limit when I realized one day that *we could no longer pay the next month's rent.* And I was seven months pregnant.

Our landlord happened to be the owner of a high-interest car loan company next door. Some people see businesses like that as loan 'sharks' because they take much higher interest than banks.

Although he was a very friendly person when you interacted with him in general, I knew he was a rigorous collector too. He would not put up with people who broke promises.

So, when I faced the fact that we couldn't possibly come up with the money for the following month's rent, I nearly panicked.

But then, I had a thought. An idea.

I looked at David and said "*I know what we can do… We can move into the kitchen!*"

So, within a couple of weeks, we moved into our commercial kitchen. Well, actually above the kitchen, between the ceiling of the kitchen structure and the tin roof of the industrial unit—a space that was used to store empty cardboard boxes and packaging materials. We created a makeshift 'home' with cardboard boxes and tarpaulins. My daughter was three years old at that time.

The security deposit we received when we moved out of our home paid another month's rent for the kitchen. On the bright side, we no longer needed to drive between our home and kitchen anymore; we were already at work when we woke up. It meant at least one more hour of sleep to me. I thought it was a great idea.

One month later, I had to face another reality; I didn't know where I was going to give birth. I was more than eight-months pregnant then. The baby could be on its way at any moment.

Luckily (and quite outlandishly), another thought came to me.

"I've done this before (given birth). So why not have the baby here? If anything unexpected happens, we could always rush to the hospital nearby."

Although I was usually the quietest person in social settings, I was also determined and quite stubborn. So, that's what happened.

On August 21, 2004 at 3:20 a.m., I delivered a healthy baby boy in our commercial kitchen in Queensland, Australia. It's clearly printed on my son's birth certificate. Seeing his peaceful face brought an overwhelming sense of joy to me.

After that, I managed to rest for three days before I got back on the 16-hour shift again with our weekend market routines. Other people at the market were surprised to see me happily working as if nothing happened. One week I was hugely pregnant, and the next I was with a newborn baby!

And to my delight, my son was a content baby who hardly ever cried as if he knew what I was dealing with, and despite the fact that his cot was a vegetable box. I felt very lucky to be able to do the work I believed in while being close to my children at the same time.

I admit that I felt stressed sometimes and occasionally felt overwhelmed. But there was an underlying feeling that I had to do what I could to keep going. Even though I could have dealt with those challenges in different ways, I didn't know any other way at that time. I trusted that it would all work out as we kept going. And I still thought that I was much better off than many people around the world who had greater challenges. That perspective was crucial.

The Real *Power of Giving*

This was a time when I experienced the real power of giving in some of the most profound ways.

When we moved to the kitchen, there was one more person who moved with us: a lovely Japanese live-in helper who was on a working holiday program. When we decided to move, we asked her to start looking for another host because we were no longer able to offer her a room to stay in.

Hearing our idea, she exuded the most beautiful smile and said, "*Wow, that's exciting! Let me move with you. I have never lived in a kitchen.*"

I don't think we could have managed what we did without her support at that time. And she still tells me now that it was one of the most remarkable life experiences she has ever had.

After that, our business started to improve. We shifted our product focus to 'Frozen Pre-Prepared Organic & Gluten-Free Meals' and began to distribute the products to many retail stores. And for this product, there was a ready market. Within a few months, we managed to move out of the kitchen and to a new home. And eventually, we started to expand our distribution to other states. We became a *national* business.

But one of the most remarkable experiences I had that related to the *Power of Giving* came in an entirely unexpected way.

One day, I turned up at the landlord's office—yes the loan 'shark' (*shhhh, don't say that! He really is a kind man.*)

I went to see him because we were once again stuck with our limited cash flow and I had to ask him to delay our rent's due date. I was already feeling very guilty about hiding the fact that we were once living in the kitchen for four months without letting him know about it. I didn't like the fact that I had something to hide when I was about to ask a favor.

So, I told him. Everything. And I told him how I believed in our business, but we needed a little more time. We were close to our breakthrough. We needed to build a proper freezer room in our kitchen to really expand our distribution.

After a few moments of silence (I nearly closed my eyes waiting for a shouting voice), I saw him crying. He then burst into laughter with tears streaming down his cheeks. He was laughing so hard that I, for the moment, laughed with him without understanding what was actually happening.

As he calmed down after a few minutes, he wiped his teary eyes and said, *"You know, Masami. I believe in you. You are a great businesswoman... You'll make it."*

I walked out of his office with the three-month rent extension and interest-free repayment terms so that we could take the time to focus on growing our business. I saw that our landlord, no matter what other people saw in him, was a very generous, sincere and caring person.

And Now...

I realize that throughout our lives, we face great challenges. Often, we have to make tough decisions. And at each point in time, we can only deal with those challenges in the ways (we think) we can. Although those decisions may not be perfect, we are likely to find next steps as we put our best intentions and care into everything we do.

Experiences like these strengthened and re-confirmed my belief that the world really is a place of incredible opportunities made possible by amazing people. And it led to my belief that each of us has the potential to care deeply, to love and to trust each other, and to create a world that's full of giving together.

I'm looking forward to what's coming ahead.

Even though nothing will ever turn out to be totally as expected.

IN GRATITUDE

The creation of this book was made possible by so many people. For me, it's a reflection of the 41 years of my life and over 20 years of my career with all the small dots finally coming together.

In the highly quoted Stanford Commencement address on June 12, 2005, Steve Jobs, then CEO of Apple Computer and of Pixar Animation Studios, reflected on his story about 'connecting the dots'. *"…you can't connect the dots looking forward; you can only connect them looking backward. So you have to trust that the dots will somehow connect in your future. You have to trust in something—your gut, destiny, life, karma, whatever. This approach has never let me down, and it has made all the difference in my life."* [43]

I've connected all the dots together in this book too. And finally, I can say that I see the meaning of every dot I've encountered. All the joys and challenges, problems we tackled, people we met and lessons we learned. Yes, now I can look backward to see the connections. And I'm grateful for the gift these small dots brought to me and to this book.

I'm grateful for the childhood I had in Japan, surrounded by the unique moral and cultural values of its long-standing history. Through difficult times as well as joyful moments when I was growing up, I learned the meaning of love and the human desire to seek our own true identity: the meaning of life. I'm grateful for my parents, family members and friends who showed me what it was like to really care and to try to become better every day, to be of greater service to others through everything we do, and to do so sincerely.

And I'm grateful for the opportunity I had to go out into the wider world after completing my education in Japan. Meeting, living and working with countless people in so many countries—people with different cultural backgrounds, with different ethnicities, with different religions and beliefs—and connecting with them in simple ways, I learned to trust and to appreciate our differences and to be open-minded and open-hearted.

I'm grateful for my children, Myra and Kai, who let me experience the unconditional love and the real joy of living each and every day, and for my ex-partner and special friend David for sharing the beginning of this business and family journey with me.

And I'm grateful for Paul, my husband, soul mate and business mentor, who has helped me express my ideas and feelings through the work we do together. It hasn't been without challenges, but it has always been joyful, meaningful and rewarding.

I'm grateful for my team at Buy1GIVE1 who works hard (joyfully) to make things happen each day. I'm grateful for the special people who are on the B1G1 Giving Board, who choose to share their time, expertise, knowledge and insight to advance our shared mission. And I'm grateful for all the people from different businesses and charity organizations that have chosen to be part of this unique giving initiative. Seeing positive impacts and so many smiles created around the world every day makes everything we do so meaningful.

I'm grateful for those who have shown us what it means to give, to care, to innovate and to improve for greatness. Because of all these amazing people, this book exists.

And finally, I'm grateful for you, for picking up this book and for spending your precious time to explore the ideas expressed here.

I hope those ideas and this book have added extra meaning to your day, to your life and to your work.

Once again, thank you for choosing to read this book, GIVING BUSINESS, and thank you for exploring these ideas.

I wish you a fantastic journey ahead!

In gratitude,

Masami Sato

SPECIAL TIPS FOR EVERYDAY CHALLENGES

Even after reading this book, there may be times you feel challenged, confused or stressed out.

Being a leader of a team, an organization or business is not always easy.

So, I have listed some tips that may help you to effectively deal with some common situations and challenges below. Please also feel free to send me your comments, questions and suggestions through LinkedIn: **linkedin.com/in/masamisato** or Twitter: **twitter.com/masamisato**

> **Please note**: *The ideas listed below are not designed to fix your problems. In reality, you are the only person who can overcome your own challenges and find great meaning in doing so. So, these recommendations are only intended to help you find new perspectives in certain challenging situations. If you are in the best state of mind, you'll always find a way to create the best outcome in your own unique way.*

When you feel down or depressed

Taking anti-depressant drugs, eating chocolate or drinking alcohol is the last thing you should consider doing when you feel down or depressed, even though these things may give you an instant high.

There is usually an underlying cause for our feelings. So, instant relief by an external aid (like a magic pill) never solves the real problem deep down. And by covering up the real issue by having an external stimulus repeatedly may make you dependent on that stimulus over time—yes, an addiction, for example. And these habits can create more persistent depression in the long run.

If you want another type of quick relief in a more holistic way, without the adverse side effects, it's more effective to do things inspired people would do.

Going out for a walk, conversing positively with others, reading an inspiring book, eating healthy food, going out in the sun, keeping busy serving others, listening to uplifting music, trying new things and so on. There are so many things you can do to instantly get out of a dark mood. And these things are actually as easy as popping a pill into your mouth.

Know that it is ok to feel down, and to be a bit moody at times. We are all human, and we cannot be the 'perfect leader' all the time. If you need to, let others know that you are not feeling so great today so that you will have extra support and acceptance from others around you. And remember that having some dark days help us to become more tolerant and understanding of others' challenges.

When you are upset about certain situations

In my earlier book, 'Joy—the Gift of Acceptance, Trust and Love', I wrote about this simple equation that transforms any situation.

"Acceptance (of the past) + Trust (in the future) = Love (present)"

If we can first accept everything, every person and every situation (because you cannot change what has already happened anyway) and trust the future (because you actually never know what will happen in the future), we can experience more joy—the love for everything and everyone—in the present moment. It helps you experience the most joy in your business, and it unleashes the power of your creative mind too. Any problems can be turned into great opportunities when you are in this state of mind.

If you want a free copy of the e-book, JOY, you can send me a message through **twitter.com/masamisato** requesting 'The JOY Book'.

When you are unwell

Everything always happens for a reason. Sickness, along with other things in life, occur for a reason too.

At times, drugs and surgeries may give you a quicker relief especially in emergency health situations. They may even save your life. We are very fortunate to be living in this world where our advanced medical procedures can protect us from conditions that were regarded as death sentences in the past.

However, real solutions to chronic health issues cannot be brought into your life without your own effort and continuous improvement (refer to the Success Funnel on page 116).

It's definitely helpful to seek advice and support from experienced health practitioners in your healing process. But you also need to make your own effort to understand what is happening in your body. A lot of health issues that people have are created as a result of their lifestyle habits and long-standing emotional imbalances.

Having great health and vitality allows you to perform consistently at your best. It means that caring for your own body is much more important than something you do just for your own benefit. It's one of the most important responsibilities for you to fulfill in order to live the greatest giving life.

When you have financial difficulties

Interestingly, the reason we experience certain financial and business challenges is also because of underlying situations we have created in life and business in many cases.

So, unless you identify the cause and work towards overcoming those challenges, you are likely to attract similar kind of challenges again and again.

Sometimes, external conditions that are out of your control might affect your financial situation both negatively and positively. Those are great times when you can review the financial strengths (or weaknesses) you've created. And if you have created strong relationships with others, stable emotional balance, and good health, most financial challenges can be solved.

If you are experiencing detrimental issues that can (in your perception) destroy your life and career entirely, then you need to review how you are building other areas of your life as well.

Getting external help with your financial challenges can bring a quicker and easier solution to your current problem, and sometimes it is extremely useful. If you receive support from others, it is important that you find ways to pay back, and forward. But the most important thing is to understand our challenges and improve our approach so that we can create a better, stronger and more impactful life.

When you have relationship issues

The source of most relationship issues starts with judgment. It's either one person judging the other, or both judging each other. When we remove judgment from the discussion or situation, most challenges are easy to solve. We can always find common ground and a win-win solution. Therefore, before you start thinking that you have a relationship problem, you can look at where your judgment lies and how to perceive and interpret the situation without any judgment.

This is not easy to do in some cases. However, it is usually the only way to the real solution and understanding.

If you tried to understand and respect the other person's views and tried your best to come up with a direction that serves both of you, you will likely get better cooperation and outcomes. And it is useful to understand that the actions, words, and behaviors of others are also often driven by other challenges the person is experiencing. If you see this as a game, then you need to find ways to create situations where the whole game becomes more enjoyable for everyone who is playing.

And after all, you are not here to *fix* everyone's problems either. The problems we face are great gifts that we are given to learn from and grow with. So, it is also okay for you to choose move on and play the game with the people who support you in achieving your goal, and who make you become a better person by sharing the journey. It is great to always help each other as much as we can, but letting others deal with their own challenges at their own pace is sometimes beneficial for everyone in the game.

When you don't feel the meaning in your work

When you cannot feel meaning in what you do (even when you *know* it), you are likely looking for something big; something great and significant so that you can appreciate what you do.

This often happens when we compare our own situation with someone else's—something that seems much better and greater.

The thing is, all you need to know is the importance of what you are doing right now. No matter how small, it's a step forward for you to reach the next great milestone. So, even if you cannot really feel the connection to a great purpose or significant direction, you can still focus on doing your best with what you are doing now.

Even simple paperwork, data entry or a customer conversation can suddenly have more meaning when you perceive it as one great opportunity to make an improvement and a new connection. Again, as Steve Jobs said, *"You can only connect the dots when you look backward and not forward."*

And if this doesn't work, it could be time for you to review what you are doing, so that you can re-align your actions with the direction you really want to head towards.

When others don't get your idea

The reason others don't *get* your idea is either that you are not expressing it clearly, or your idea is actually not so great (even though it can become better with articulation).

And there is nothing personal about this. Unless you are in a social circle where judgment is distorting actual reality, what you see in others' reactions gives you an indication of the quality of your communication: either how you are communicating or what you are communicating.

When you understand this and stay open-minded, you can easily accept and be grateful for other people's inputs whether they are positive or negative. And remember that novices appreciate negative criticism to get better (see page 58). So, by eagerly receiving both negative and positive feedback with an open mind, you are becoming a real expert.

....

And if you still have difficulty feeling positive and inspired, you can simply think of those who have greater challenges than you, read about their stories or even do spontaneous giving by jumping on to **www. b1g1.com/projects**. You may find relief from all kinds of challenges by knowing that you've just added extra meaning and joy to someone else's day.

WISHING YOU A GREAT BUSINESS JOURNEY
FULL OF MEANING AND POSITIVE IMPACTS.

ABOUT MASAMI SATO

Masami Sato is a social entrepreneur, CEO and founder of the global giving initiative, Buy1GIVE1 (B1G1), and author of three books: '**JOY**—The Gift of Acceptance, Trust and Love', '**ONE**—Sharing the Joy of Giving' and '**GIVING BUSINESS**—Creating the maximum impact in a meaning-driven world'. She is also a mother of two children and is a two-time TEDx speaker.

Masami's unique insights and methodologies are cultivated from the mixture of her Japanese heritage and her diverse experiences traveling around the world, working in many different industries and countries. Her keen interest and appreciation for different philosophies, concepts and ideologies of our world combined with her practical business experience has helped form the new and innovative ways B1G1 allows businesses and individuals to give and impact lives today. Since its founding in 2007, businesses and individuals working with B1G1 have created more than 78 million giving impacts.

You can find out more about B1G1 at **www.b1g1.com** and integrate effective giving in your life and business too. For more information or to invite Masami to speak at your event, you can contact the B1G1 Team via **connect@b1g1.com**.

A Small Gift of Giving...

For every five copies of GIVING BUSINESS that is purchased, one native tree is planted and nurtured in Borneo to reduce effects of deforestation and help protect Orangutans. Thank you for being a part of GIVING BUSINESS.

REFERENCES

Many parts of this book contain references to various studies and information found through other organization's websites and literature. To give you the full picture of where they come from and access to extra information associated with the facts and figures, we have listed the names of studies and/or links to those sources below. We also recognize people and organizations for their effort in collecting, collating and analyzing the data and information that matters.

(Endnotes)

1.   'In It Together: Why Less Inequality Benefits All' by OECD: http://www. oecd-ilibrary.org/

2.   'AN ECONOMY FOR THE 1%' by Oxfam: https://www.oxfam.org

3.   'INTERNET USAGE STATISTICS 2015' by Internet World Stats: http:// www.internetworldstats.com/ and 'Our History' (2015) by Facebook: http://newsroom.fb.com/company-info/

4.   'Global Water Crisis: Water And Sanitation Facts' by http://water.org/

5.   '2015 Cone Communication/Ebiquity Global CSR Study' by Cone Communications: http://www.conecomm.com/

6.   'Poll of Established Adults Ages 25-39' by Clark University: http://www. clarku.edu/

7.   'The Wisdom of Bees: What the Hive Can Teach Business about Leadership, Efficiency, and Growth' by Michael O'Malley

8.   'Save the Bees' by Greenpeace: http://www.greenpeace.org/usa/sustainable-agriculture/save-the-bees/

9.   'The Culture of an Engaged Workplace' by Gallup: http://www.gallup.com

10. 'Keeping It in the Family' by Emily Tamkin on Slate: http://www.slate.com

11. 'Here is the reason why average lifespan of US corporations has never been shorter' by ZeroHedge: http://www.zerohedge.com/news/2014-12-04/here-reason-why-average-lifespan-us-corporations-has-never-been-shorter

12. '12 Challenges Faced By The Fastest-Growing Companies' by John Hall, Forbes: http://www.forbes.com

13. 'The Least Loyal Employees' by Payscale: http://www.payscale.com/data-packages/employee-loyalty/least-loyal-employees

14. Mission statement of Google (as of 2016): http://www.google.com/intl/us/about/

15. Mission statement of Apple (as of 2015): http://investor.apple.com/

16. Mission statement of McDonald's (as of 2016): http://www.aboutmcdonalds.com

17. Mission statement of IKEA (as of 2016): http://www.ikea.com/

18. Mission statement of American Express (as of 2016): http://americanexpress.com/oc/whoweare/

19. Mission statement of Patagonia (as of 2016): http://www.patagonia.com/us/home

20. Mission/Vision statement of Unilever (as of 2016): https://www.unilever.com/

21. 'Start with WHY' by Simon Sinek: https://www.startwithwhy.com

22. 'What You Really Need to Lead: The Power of Thinking and Acting Like an Owner' by Robert Steven Kaplan

23. 'How Positive and Negative Feedback Motivate Goal Pursuit' by Ayelet Fishbach1, Tal Eyal, Stacey R. Finkelstein: http://onlinelibrary.wiley.com

24. 'Praise for Intelligence Can Undermine Children's Motivation and Performance' by Claudia Mueller and Carol Dweck: https://psychology.stanford.edu

25. 'The Firm of Future' by Paul Dunn and Ronald J. Baker: http://www.amazon.com/The-Firm-Future-Accountants-Professional/dp/0471264245

26. 'Meaningful' by Barnadette Jiwa: http://meaningfulbook.com/

27. 'The Starbucks Mission Statement and Corporate Social Responsibility': http://www.starbucks.com/responsibility

28. 'Prosocial Spending and Happiness: Using Money to Benefit Others Pays Off' by Dunn, Elizabeth W., Lara B. Aknin, and Michael I. Norton: http://www.hbs.edu

29. 'Social Business' defined by Prof. Muhammad Yunus: https://en.wikipedia.org/wiki/Social_business

30. Giving Impacts by B1G1 Members: https://www.businessesforgood.com

31. 'Maslow's Hierarchy of Needs'—a theory from 'A Theory of Human Motivation' by Abraham Maslow, 1943

32. 'Connected—The surprising power of our Social Networks' by Nicholas A. Christakis and James H. Fowler: http://www.connectedthebook.com/

33. 'Surprising Facts and Stats About The Big Data Industry' (2015) by Daniel Price on CloudTweaks: http://cloudtweaks.com/

34. A survey conducted by PNC Wealth Management: https://www.pnc.com

35. A study and analytics based on Gallup-Healthways Well-Being Index (GHWBI) survey by Angus Deaton, Ph.D. and Daniel Kahneman, Ph.D.: http://www.gallup.com

36. Global Statistics by UNICEF: http://www.unicef.org/statistics/

37. WHO global water and sanitation statistics: http://www.who.int/water_sanitation_health/wsh0404summary/en/

38. UNESCO global statistics: http://en.unesco.org

39. 'Poverty Facts and Stats' by GLOBAL ISSUES: http://www.globalissues.org/article/26/poverty-facts-and-stats

40. Industry size statistics as of 2016 by IBIS World: http://www.ibisworld.com

41. How B1G1 Projects are selected: https://www.b1g1.com/businessforgood/worthy-cause-programme/

42. B1G1 Projects Examples: https://www.b1g1.com/projects

43. Steve Jobs' Stanford Commencement Speech (2005): http://news.stanford.edu/news/2005/june15/jobs-061505.html

66962058R00111

Made in the USA
Charleston, SC
02 February 2017